I0797511

The Blood Libel in Medieval Antisemitism

PAST IMPERFECT

Further Information and Publications

www.arc-humanities.org/series/book-series/

The Blood Libel in Medieval Antisemitism

François Soyer

British Library Cataloguing in Publication Data

A catalogue record for this book is available from the British Library.

ISBN (print) 9781802701807
e-ISBN (PDF) 9781802703627
e-ISBN (EPUB) 9781802703634

www.arc-humanities.org

Printed and bound in the UK (by CPIGroup [UK] Ltd), USA (by Bookmasters), and elsewhere using print-on-demand technology.

Publisher (manufacturer) details: Arc Humanities Press, 14 Clifton Moor Business Village, James Nicolson Link, York YO30 4XG, United Kingdom.

EU Authorized Representative details (for GPSR purposes): Amsterdam University Press, Nieuwe Prinsengracht 89, 1018 VR Amsterdam, The Netherlands. www.aup.nl

In memory of
Bjorn Weiler (1969–2024)

Professor of Medieval History
at the University of Aberystwyth
and dearly missed friend

Contents

List of Illustrations

Introduction

In 1543, the famous German theologian and Protestant reformer Martin Luther published an infamous polemical attack on the Jews entitled *On the Jews and their Lies*. Luther appealed for a range of oppressive measures against Jews, including the destruction of synagogues and religious schools as well as the confiscation of "their prayer books and Talmudic writings." Luther represented Jews not just as obdurate in their refusal to convert to Christianity but also as a danger to the lives of all Christians. They were, Luther raged, taught by the Talmud (the rabbinical writings on Jewish law and traditions) to hate Christians and, whenever the opportunity arose, sought to kill Christian children:

> Therefore, dear Christian, be advised and do not doubt that next to the Devil, you have no more bitter, venomous, and vehement foe than a real Jew who earnestly seeks to be a Jew. ... the history books often accuse them of contaminating wells, of kidnapping and piercing children, as for example at Trent, Weissensee, etc. They, of course, deny this. Whether it is true or not, I do know that they do not lack the complete, full and ready will to do such things either secretly or openly where possible.

Later in his work, the accusation of child-killing appeared a second time:

> Thus, they have been accused of poisoning water and wells, of kidnapping children, of piercing them through with an

> awl, of hacking them to pieces, and in that way secretly cooling their wrath with the blood of Christians, for all of which they have often been condemned to death by fire.[1]

Luther does not provide much detail about the accusation of child murder. Moreover, he was careful to avoid personally proclaiming the truth of such accusations, even though he suggested that they were credible. The accusation was not an invention of Luther's but rather a well-established medieval libel against Jews. Indeed, the claim that Jews abducted and murdered Christian children either to stage insulting parodies of Christ's Passion, to concoct magical or medicinal potions, or even to consume their blood during Passover constitutes the most extreme of all the libels used to attack Jews and present them as an existential threat to Christians. From twelfth-century England, where the allegation first surfaced, the child murder libel has been a staple of extreme antisemitic discourse seeking to dehumanize Jews and rationalize anti-Jewish violence.

The child murder libel encompasses a range of different accusations given different names. This book uses the broad notion of "child murder libel" instead of "ritual murder" to refer to the general medieval accusation that Jews abducted and killed Christian children in religiously motivated murders. The phrase "ritual murder" has become a blanket term commonly employed by historians to refer to these child murder libels and German historians refer to the "ritual murder legend" (*Ritualmordlegende*). It is, however, a modern expression derived from the German phrase *Ritualmord* that the Hungarian parliamentarian and antisemitic agitator Géza von Ónody coined in 1882. Nineteenth-century antisemites co-opted the term "ritual" to argue that the accusation had a scientific basis in academic anthropology and was therefore credible. The historian Gavin Langmuir has distinguished

1 Martin Luther, "On the Jews and Their Lies," in *Luther's Works*, vol. 47, ed. Franklin Sherman and Helmut T. Lehmann (Philadelphia: Fortress, 1971), 217 and 264.

between two separate child murder libels. The first, "ritual crucifixion" or "crucifixion murder," is the claim that Jews ritually crucify children, usually at Easter, to parody the crucifixion of Christ. The second, "blood libel," "blood accusation," or even "ritual cannibalism," is the accusation that Jews collect the blood of a Christian child in order to consume it, usually as part of the Passover festival. In practice, a stark distinction between accusations of "ritual crucifixion" and "blood libel" is unhelpful. It does not reflect the fact that there was sometimes overlap between the two or that, in some instances, the accusations involved neither explicit references to "ritual" purposes nor the consumption of blood. Unfortunately, some historians continue to use "ritual murder" and "blood libel" interchangeably without much regard for this important nuance.

This book offers both a critical survey of the development of the child murder libel in medieval Europe before 1500 as well as an analysis of its history. Why did the accusation appear in some areas of medieval Europe and not others? What local factors contributed to some accusations receiving support from religious or lay authorities and resulting in saintly cults despite papal condemnation? How have modern historians and sociologists explained the phenomenon? To answer these questions, this book is divided into six chapters.

Chapter 1, "The Genesis of the Child Murder Libel in Twelfth-Century Europe," discusses the rise of the accusation that Jews kidnapped and murdered Christian children, allegedly to ritually parody the Crucifixion of Christ. Starting with the case of "Saint" William of Norwich in England during the 1140s, it also examines other cases in England and France before 1300.

Chapter 2, "The Birth of the 'Blood Libel' and the Thirteenth-Century Papal Reaction," analyzes the important change that the accusation underwent in the thirteenth century. Starting at Fulda in the German lands of the Holy Roman Empire in 1235, Jews were accused of murdering children in order to consume their blood during the Passover festival or use it for medicinal or magical reasons. This created a new version of the child murder narrative. This chapter explains why this was an important change and explores the reaction of the Christian authorities. Indeed, both the Holy Roman Emperor Frederick II and the papacy condemned the blood libel accusation. Nevertheless, these condemnations failed to prevent the spread of the accusation. The chapter also examines other accusations of "ritual murder" and blood libel in the thirteenth century, including that of Lincoln in 1255 ("Little Saint Hugh"). Not a blood libel, the Lincoln accusation followed the original "ritual murder" pattern but introduced elements that linked Jews to "black magic" and witchcraft.

Chapter 3, "Simon of Trent (1475): Apex of the Blood Libel," focuses on the notorious blood libel that targeted the small Jewish community of Trent, a small Alpine town on the borders of the Holy Roman Empire and Italy, which was accused of murdering a young boy named Simon in order to consume his blood in the Passover festival. The trial that followed saw the Jews of Trent accused and convicted of the murder and the story of "Saint Simon of Trent" achieved considerable fame. The papacy initially resisted the rise of the cult of "Saint" Simon but eventually offered recognition to the saintly cult in 1588 (although it never officially canonized him as a saint). This chapter seeks to explain why the trials at Trent took place (i.e., why the local ruler supported it despite earlier papal condemnation), why the papacy eventually supported the cult of "Saint" Simon and why it achieved such notoriety. The chapter also emphasizes the role of the printing press in disseminating news and images of the story across large parts of Europe.

Chapter 4, "El Santo Niño de la Guardia: The Child Murder Libel in Iberia," analyzes another infamous case: that of the "Holy Child" (*Santo Niño*) of La Guardia in central Spain. While the blood libel of Simon of Trent has become the most notorious trial in medieval Europe, Jewish converts to Christianity (*conversos*) and Jews in fifteenth-century Spain were accused of kidnapping a toddler and murdering him in 1489 in a conspiracy to produce a magic potion that would kill all the Christians of Spain. The involvement of the Spanish Inquisition resulted in the trial and conviction of the accused and the birth of a saintly cult that endures to this day. This chapter examines how this Iberian child murder narrative was very different from that of Simon of Trent and what this difference reveals about the malleable nature of the child murder libel.

Chapter 5, "Medieval Echoes in Modern Times: The Legacy of the Child Murder Libel," examines how the medieval "ritual murder" and "blood libel" accusations disappeared from most of Western and Central Europe after the Protestant Reformation but still survived in Eastern Europe and resurfaced as an element of antisemitic discourse in the modern era. In the nineteenth century, the accusation rose to prominence once again and led to a series of trials that received sensational media coverage in Central and Eastern Europe (Germany, Hungary, and Bohemia) and, finally, in the Russian Empire in 1911–1913. This chapter examines why the accusation reappeared and whether these modern accusations and cases can be compared to the medieval ones. Indeed, a key difference is that the modern trials sought to establish the "truth" behind the blood libel through modern science.

Finally, Chapter 6, "The Attempts of Historians and Sociologists to Explain the Phenomenon," surveys and analyzes the different ways that historians and sociologists have sought to explain the phenomenon. Since each case/accusation had a specific local context, is it possible to argue that wider religious or social trends also played a role? Was the child murder accusation tied to an increasingly Christocentric Latin Christianity that emerged in Western/Latin Christendom during the twelfth century? Was the blood libel linked to a rising belief in witchcraft in the later Middle Ages? Is it just a part of antisemitic folklore or a conspiracy theory like any other? This chapter debates the merits of these different interpretations.

Chapter 1

The Genesis of the Child Murder Libel in Twelfth-Century Europe

Thomas of Monmouth, a monk of Norwich Cathedral Priory in the east of England, wrote a work entitled *The Life and Passion of William of Norwich* between 1150 and 1173. This work is an account of the death and posthumous miracles of a twelve-year-old English boy named William. On Easter Saturday William's body was discovered in a wood outside Norwich after he had disappeared. Thomas claims that those who found the boy noted "unusual" signs of torture and concluded "from the nature of the wounds that no Christian but only a Jew would have taken it upon himself to kill the innocent child in this way with such rash daring." The Christian inhabitants of the city of Norwich spent Easter Sunday in a state of uproar as "zeal of pious fervour incited everyone towards the destruction of the Jews." Thomas claims that a massacre of Norwich's Jewish community might well have ensued but that the Jews bribed the sheriff of the town to intervene to maintain the peace and protect them.

Thomas of Monmouth was not a mere chronicler recording historical events. His work is a hagiography: a reverent biography of William and account of his alleged posthumous miracles. Thomas endorses the story of William's murder by the Jews of Norwich, claiming that the boy was abducted, gruesomely tortured, crucified, and finally murdered by the Jewish community of Norwich "in mockery of the Passion of the Cross" on Good Friday in 1144. Thomas told his readers that this was not an isolated murder but that a monk named

Theobald, who was a convert from Judaism, had told him of the existence of a conspiracy of all European Jews, whose leaders regularly gathered in the southern French town of Narbonne:

> He told us that in the ancient writings of their ancestors it was written that Jews could not achieve their freedom or ever return to the lands of their fathers without the shedding of human blood. Hence it was decided by them a long time ago that every year, to the shame and affront of Christ, a Christian somewhere on earth be sacrificed to the Highest God, and so they take revenge for the injuries of Him, whose death is the reason for their exclusion from their fatherland and their exile as slaves in foreign lands.
>
> Therefore, the leaders and rabbis of the Jews who dwell in Spain, at Narbonne, where the seed of kings and their glory flourishes greatly, meet together, and cast lots of all the regions where Jews lived. Whichever region was chosen by lot, its capital city had to apply that lot to the other cities and towns and the one whose name comes up will carry out that business, as decreed. In that year, however, when William, the glorious martyr of God, was killed, it so happened that the lot fell on the men of Norwich, and all the communities of Jews of England offered their consent by letters or by messengers for the crime to be performed at Norwich.[1]

The *Life and Passion of William of Norwich* goes on to describe the miraculous discovery and burial of William's body in Norwich cathedral as well as the numerous miracles ascribed to the child martyr. Thomas of Monmouth's work is not the only nor even necessarily the earliest source for the story of William although it is by far the most detailed. An entry in the *Anglo-Saxon Chronicle*, for instance, briefly notes that "the Jews of Norwich bought a Christian child before Easter and

1 Thomas of Monmouth, *The Life and Passion of William of Norwich*, 61–62. For full details of citations which are abbreviated across the text and notes, please consult the Further Reading. Where an author is cited more than once in the Further Reading, an abbreviated title is included alongside their name in the text.

tortured him with all the same torture with which our Lord was tortured; and on Good Friday they hanged him on a rood on account of our Lord."[2]

Thomas of Monmouth's rendering of William's life follows the conventional literary scheme of many medieval martyrdom narratives. The Christian martyr attracts the hatred of non-Christians, suffers a violent death, and is secretly buried; but their mortal remains are miraculously rediscovered and reburied in a place where they perform miracles. Beyond its hagiographical nature, the narrative assumes the form of a classic conspiracy theory: a group of conspirators within society develop a secret plan to achieve a secret objective and a trustworthy inside source (the convert Theobald) reveals their nefarious plot. The story of William of Norwich does not accuse a single Jew or even just the Jewish community of Norwich of a religiously motivated murder. In the story, at least the version of Thomas of Monmouth, it is the Jews of Christian Europe, collectively, who are responsible for the murder of William. The tale accuses a Jewish elite in "Spain" of planning and coordinating the murder of a Christian child every year in order to fulfil an injunction found in the "ancient writings of their ancestors." Monmouth's claim that the Jewish community of Narbonne—a town in southern France, close to the border with Catalonia in Spain—was the centre of a Jewish conspiracy to murder Christians is linked to legends and rumours apparently circulating in England and continental Europe at the time. There did exist a prosperous Jewish community in twelfth-century Narbonne and Jewish authors describe its elite as claiming descent from King David and enjoying an exalted position within the Jewish diaspora. Christian authors apparently picked this up. Writing in the 1140s, the respected abbot Peter the Venerable of Cluny in France referred to a "king of the Jews" in Narbonne in his anti-Jewish polemic *Against the Inveterate Obduracy of the Jews.*

---

2 Michael Swanton, ed. and trans., *The Anglo-Saxon Chronicle* (London: Routledge, 1998), 265.

Likewise, the twelfth-century English monk William of Malmesbury claimed that there existed an enormously wealthy Jewish religious dignitary in Narbonne who was the *summum papa* ("highest pope") of the Jews and that all the Jews in the world obeyed his legal pronouncements.[3] In Thomas of Monmouth's narrative, the Jews of Narbonne do not explicitly seek to have a child killed but rather just "a Christian somewhere on earth." The Jews of Norwich select William as their victim not because he is a child but rather because he was well known to the Jews, for whom he had allegedly performed repairs on mantles, furs, and other items of clothing, and this familiarity facilitated his abduction.

The significance of the claim that the Jews of Norwich abducted a Christian child and murdered him in a parody of the Passion of Christ lies in the fact that William de Turbeville, the bishop of Norwich between ca. 1146 and 1174, supported the cult. The bishop, to whom Thomas of Monmouth dedicated his hagiography, appears to have hoped to establish Norwich as a pilgrimage site and the story spread rapidly in England and on the continent. The bishop oversaw the translation of William's body into the cathedral and its reburial under an altar dedicated to holy martyrs. While there is only a single surviving manuscript of Thomas of Monmouth's hagiography of William, the story clearly circulated as it was retold, presumably both orally and in written form. The links between monastic houses appear to have assisted in this process. William already appeared in the calendar of saints' feast days in monasteries as far away as Bavaria during the 1140s (Monmouth, xvii, 3–7, 146–47).

The exact transmission and spread of William of Norwich's story to other parts of England and continental Europe is difficult to trace with any degree of accuracy. It would be tempting to ascribe it to pilgrims, but the evidence indicates that the cult was very localized and drew mostly local folk from

---

3 Peter the Venerable, *Against the Inveterate Obduracy of the Jews*, ed. and trans. Irven M. Resnick (Washington, DC: The Catholic University of America Press, 2013), 140.

Figure 1. Depiction on a rood screen of the crucifixion of William, fifteenth century. Holy Trinity Church, Loddon, Norfolk. Holmes Garden Photos/Alamy Stock Photo. Used with permission.

the counties of Norfolk and Suffolk. Nevertheless, other accusations of religiously motivated child murder by Jews began to appear in England during the second half of the twelfth century. The discovery of the mutilated body of a child in the River Severn in 1168 led to the spread of rumours that he had been murdered by Jews. Unfortunately, there is no surviving contemporary source for this case similar to Thomas of Monmouth's life of William. A thirteenth-century chronicle only notes that "at this Easter a certain boy was crucified at Gloucester" but gives the date of 1161. Details of the story only appear in a very brief entry in a history of the monastery of Saint Peter in Gloucester written between 1382 and 1412. According to this source, which admits that "no Christian was present or saw or heard these torments, nor have we found that anything was discovered from any Jew," a child named Harold was "carried secretly away by Jews in the opinion of many" and murdered by "the Jews of all England" who had gathered in the town, ostensibly to celebrate the circumcision of a Jewish child. The narrative claims that the Jews gruesomely tortured the boy, who allegedly had wounds on his head indicating that he had been made to wear a crown of thorns like Christ, and that "they had made him a glorious martyr to Christ" (Hillaby, 75–80).

Nearer to Norwich, in the Suffolk town of Bury St. Edmunds, another child murder libel appeared in 1181 in the form of the cult of Robert of Bury. Just like Harold of Gloucester, the extant evidence is sparse. The English chronicler and monk of Bury St. Edmunds Jocelin of Brakelond, who wrote between 1173 and 1202, briefly mentions that in the year 1181 "the saintly boy Robert was martyred and was buried in our church: many signs and wonders were performed among the people, as I have recorded elsewhere." Jocelin's other account of Robert's "martyrdom" has not been found but another contemporary monastic chronicler, Gervase of Canterbury, states that "[in 1181] the Jews martyred a boy at Easter" in Bury St. Edmunds and that the child-martyr was buried in the abbey and performing miracles. Apart from these terse sources, little else is known about the legend and martyrdom narrative of Robert of Bury St. Edmunds. A much later rhyming "Prayer to Saint Robert" was penned by John Lydgate of Bury (ca. 1370–ca. 1451), a native of Suffolk who was also a monk of Bury St. Edmunds as well as a poet. Lydgate refers in his short prayer to the "story" of Robert—presumably a *Vita* or Passion narrative—to allege that the Jews scourged and crucified the child. It would be tempting to see the rise of the cult of "Saint" Robert as the result of the rivalry between the abbey of Bury St. Edmunds and the cathedral of Norwich, which fostered its own cult of "Saint" William. Such an interpretation, however, ignores the fact that the story of Robert emerged in the context of a local power struggle within the abbey between two senior monks: Samson the subsacristan and his rival the sacristan William. This struggle apparently stoked anti-Jewish feeling. Jocelin de Brakelond claims that William enjoyed the support of many Christians as well as "the Jews, I say, to whom the sacristan was said to be a father and a patron." It was Samson who emerged the victor and became abbot in 1182 yet, Jocelin notes elsewhere in his work, "wheresoever the abbot went, there hastened to him both Jews and Christians demanding payment of the debts due to them." Is the libel tied to this power struggle, with which it coincides? This certainly seems possible, and Abbot Samson eventually secured royal authorization to expel the Jews from Bury although Jocelin does not mention a direct connection between the cult of Saint Robert and the expulsion in his chronicle.[4]

In the south of England, another contemporary chronicler named Richard of Devizes alleged that circa 1192 the Jews of the town of Winchester murdered an orphaned boy of French origin at Passover. The boy was an apprentice to a cobbler and his age is not specified. Richard of Devizes claims that the Jews chose the boy because, like William of Norwich in Thomas of Monmouth's narrative, he often visited Jews. In the story, a friend of the boy inquires about his disappearance

4 Jocelin of Brakelond, *Chronicle of the Abbey of Bury St Edmunds* (Oxford: Oxford University Press, 1998), 3–4, 6–7, 10, and 15.

and causes a tumult when he accuses the Jews of crucifying the boy and eating him. A Christian woman who cared for Jewish children comes forth to claim that she has witnessed the boy go down into a Jew's underground storeroom but never re-emerge. Like Thomas of Monmouth before him, Richard of Devizes ends his story by accusing the Jews of bribing local judges to dismiss the case.[5]

A major issue for historians is that there is no surviving contemporary hagiographical text for either Harold of Gloucester or Robert of Bury St. Edmunds comparable to the *Life of William of Norwich* by Thomas of Monmouth. In a comprehensive study of the evidence relating to the story of Harold of Gloucester, Joe Hillaby has persuasively argued that the material used in the history of the monastery of Saint Peter in Gloucester centuries later "indicates that the story of Harold must, ultimately, have been drawn from a contemporary *Life*." This text has either been destroyed or remains undiscovered. Jocelin of Brakelond apparently wrote a hagiographical *Life* of Robert which is now lost. A fifteenth-century manuscript version of the text, possibly a summary of it, still existed in the twentieth century but trace of it has been lost after its sale at auction in 1959.

Just as accusations of child murder targeting Jews were spreading in England, they were also emerging in continental Europe, more precisely across the English Channel in France. How the accusation of child murder spread is unclear. It is tempting to think that the bishop of Norwich actively promoted the cult and story of William of Norwich in a fundraising tour of France with the boy's relics but, until definite evidence appears, such a claim remains tantalizingly conjectural (Rose, 151–85). It is just as possible that monks, pilgrims, merchants, and other travellers disseminated it. Regardless of precisely how the child murder accusation spread, it was

5 *The Chronicle of Richard of Devizes: Concerning the Deeds of Richard the First, King of England. Also, Richard of Cirencester's Description of Britain*, trans. J. A. Giles (London: Bohn, 1841), 62–64.

definitely present in France in the 1170s, even before the accusation in Bury St. Edmunds.

For the first time, the child murder accusation led to the deaths of Jews and is recorded in contemporary Jewish sources when it was levelled against the Jews of the town of Blois in western France. One Jewish writer claims that a Christian accused a Jew watering his horse by a river and carrying an untanned hide of disposing of the body of "a little Christian child, whom the Jews had killed." Although no body was found and no bereaved parents came forth to report a missing child, the accusation led to the execution of thirty Jews, male and female, by burning at the stake. The Jewish sources provide scant details about the accusation beyond the alleged murder. Robert of Torigni, the Abbot of Mont-Saint-Michel between 1154 and 1186, also records that in the year 1171 many Jews were burnt at Blois. He is explicit about the religious motivation, stating that "a child was killed by many Jews who, to show their contempt of Christians, had crucified a child at Easter. Afterwards they put him into a sack and threw him into the River Loire." Robert was well aware of the English legends of William of Norwich and Harold of Gloucester. For him the credibility of the affair at Blois was strengthened because "during the reign of King Stephen, at Norwich in England, they did the same thing to Saint William: he was buried in the cathedral there and many miracles are performed at his shrine. The same thing happened to another [child] at Gloucester in the time of King Henry II." Robert concludes that "frequently, as it is said, they do this in the Easter season, if they find an opportunity" ("Et frequenter, ut dicitur, faciunt hoc in tempore Paschali, si opportunitatem invenerint"). Modern historians have noted that the horrifying incident occurred against a background of rising tension between the Jews of Blois and the lord of the town, Count Theobald, who appears to have welcomed an excuse to seize the property of the victims.[6]

---

6 "Robert of Torigni: Chronicle," in *Chronicles of the Reigns of Stephen, Henry II and Richard I*, ed. Richard Howlett, vol. 4, Rerum

The judicial massacre at Blois was the first massacre directly attributable to the child murder libel in the twelfth century but it was not the only such accusation in France. Another child murder narrative emerged around the same time in the form of the alleged martyrdom of Richard of Pontoise (a locality to the northwest of Paris), also known as Richard of Paris. The dating of this accusation varies according to different sources. The author of the Annals of Cambrai, which end in 1170, is our earliest known source and dates it to the year 1163, tersely noting that "that year, in Paris, on the day of the celebration of the Passion of Christ, the Jews crucified an adolescent Christian named Richard out of disdain for Christ" ("Iudaei apud Parisios eodem anno in die celebrationis passionis Domini quemdam adolescentem christianum nomine Richardum ob Christi despectum cruci affixerunt"). Abbot Robert of Torigni mentions "Saint Richard" in passing while discussing the affair at Blois in 1171, merely recording that he had suffered "a similar death" (i.e., crucifixion) at the hands of the "impious Jews."[7]

Our knowledge of the legend of Richard of Pontoise/Paris is heavily dependent on *The Passion of Richard the Martyr* (*Passio sancti Richardi martyris*), a funeral oration written in 1498 by Robert Gaguin, humanist writer and minister general of the Trinitarian Order. Gaguin's hagiographic narrative claims that the Jews were consumed by a "never-ending hatred" (*perpetuum odium*) of Christians and "were accustomed to killing a Christian every year" ("consuetudinem fecerint quotannis dam occidendi quempiam christianum") and that the young Richard was lured by them into an underground passageway. Gaguin's version of the *Passio* has a rabbi question Richard about his faith, to which the boy defiantly reaffirms his belief in "Jesus, born of the Virgin Mary

Britannicarum Medii Aevi Scriptores (London: Eyre and Spottiswoode, 1889), 250–51.

7 Axelle Neyrinck, "Richard de Pontoise: Le 'saint Innocent' parisien," *Histoire urbaine* 60, no. 1 (2021): 67.

through the Holy Spirit and who was branded with rods and spit upon by your race, and condemned to a vile death, he so pure and innocent, in order to redeem the human race and bring it back from hell to rest in the kingdom of God the Father, of whom He is the only son." Richard, Gaguin relates, then suffered torture and abuse similar to Christ's during his Passion:

> Immediately, the faithful Richard was undressed, beaten with fists, and scourged most horribly with rods. The Jews mocking him, and in his person reviling and blaspheming Jesus and His mother Mary, and cursing Him in Richard's face, although they marvelled at his patience and constancy.[8]

The boy endures his suffering with the typical exemplarity of the Christian martyr, singing the Psalm *Libera me Domine*, until the enraged Jews crucify Richard, who expires on the cross like Christ. Gaguin ends the martyrdom narrative by recounting that the boy's burial took place in the cemetery of the Holy Innocents in Paris and that he had performed miracles for those who venerated him. Such was his "fame" that the English had allegedly stolen his body (minus his head) in the fifteenth century. The absence of a surviving martyrdom narrative from the twelfth or thirteenth centuries, unfortunately, means that it is impossible to know the extent to which Gaguin's hagiography included details added later, possibly by him.

Stories and rumours of child murders committed by Jews appear to have been circulating freely in northern France in the 1170s and 1180s. Robert of Torigni also noted in his chronicle that in the year 1177 "St William was killed by the Jews of Paris" on April 21, but the body was "entirely burnt up by fire" and nothing more is known of this accusation. Another chronicler, a monk of Saint Denis named Rigord, claimed that as a child King Philip Augustus "heard many times from

8 Robert Gaguin, *Epistulae et orationes* (Paris: André Bocard pour Durand Gerlier, 1498), unpaginated.

children who had been raised with him in the palace ... that the Paris Jews were wont every year on Easter Sunday or during the week of Our Lord's Passion to go secretly down into underground vaults and kill a Christian as a sort of sacrifice, in contempt of the Christian religion." Rigord's use of the phrase *quasi pro sacrificio* is strong evidence of the claim that the death was a ritualized murder. Rigord mentions the "crucifixion" and death of Richard of Pontoise in the year 1179. William Le Breton, another contemporary chronicler, goes even further in claiming that the stories young Philip Augustus had heard were that "the Jews sacrificed a child and communed with its heart" ("immolabant, et eius corde se communicabant"). The verb *communicabant* clearly implies a belief that the Jews came together as a community to consume a child's heart in a grotesque parody of the Christian Holy Communion. Rigord suggests in his chronicle that the child murder libel helped motivate Philip Augustus' decision to expel the Jews from the French Crown's lands in 1182. The evidence, however, suggests that the cult of Robert of Pontoise was not so much the cause of the expulsion of 1182 but rather a consequence of it. Indeed, possibly inspired by the affair at Blois, Philip Augustus appears to have sought to enhance his public image by appealing to rising popular antipathy towards Jews and improve his finances by seizing Jewish property.

One last incident occurring in France during the twelfth century is worth examining. The chronicler Rigord records the burning of over eighty Jews in Bray-sur-Seine, southeast of Paris, on the orders of King Philip Augustus of France. Freshly returned from the Third Crusade, the king supposedly intervened after the local ruler allowed the Jews to mistreat a Christian whom they bound and designated as a thief and, having placed a crown of thorns on his head, hanged from a gallows. An account of the event by a twelfth-century Jewish source, Ephraim of Bonn, offers a contrasting version of the event. Ephraim of Bonn does not deny that the Jews put to death a Christian but that they did so in very different circumstances than those claimed by Rigord. In the Jewish account, the Jews seek redress from the countess for the murder of a Jew by a Christian:

> And his relatives [i.e., of the deceased Jews] came and cried out before the countess—although the murderer was a vassal of the King of France—and bribed her to hang the assassin. And they hung him on Purim (Chazan, "The Bray Incident," 6).

As Robert Chazan has pointed out, the "they" in the final sentence is ambiguous since it is unclear whether the execution was carried out by the Jews themselves (as Rigord claims) or the officials of the countess. The mention of Purim, the Jewish holiday commemorating the saving of the Jewish people from annihilation in the Persian Empire through the intervention of Esther and the hanging of the Persian official Haman, is interesting. Purim and the public festivities of Jews associated with it frequently aroused the suspicions of Christians who interpreted the mocking and "execution" of Haman in effigy as a disguised attempt to re-enact the death of Jesus and ridicule the Christian faith. Rigord presents the killing as the result of an "ancient hatred," suggesting that it was religiously motivated, but Ephraim of Bonn presents it as a criminal execution and hints that the problematic issue lay in the fact that the Christian murderer was a vassal of the king of France. Certainly, Philip Augustus' devastatingly swift and brutal intervention strongly suggests that he was punishing a slight on his royal authority as much as any perceived religious provocation. The execution at Bray and the massacre that followed it are sometimes treated as an example of a "ritual murder" accusation, but it is certainly not a child murder libel. To start with, most obviously of all, the executed Christian was not a child. Secondly, Rigord presents the Jews as motivated by an "an old hatred" (*antiquo odio commoti*) and suggestively refers to the use of a crown of thorns but there is no reference to Easter. Rigord himself does not draw any comparison with the "martyrdom" of Richard of Pontoise.

The rise of the child murder libel did not occur in a vacuum. The twelfth century witnessed the beginnings of a gradual increase in hostility against Jews in western Christendom. Popular hostility manifested itself in the anti-Jewish massacres that occurred in the 1140s in the Rhineland during the Second Crusade and well as at York in England in 1190. The hostility was not just popular but expressed by influential clergymen. The Abbot of Cluny, Peter the Venerable, told the crusading King Louis VII of France in a mid-twelfth-century letter that the Jews were worse than Muslims:

> But what value [is there] in pursuing and attacking the enemies of the Christian faith in remote and distant lands while the Jews, wretched blasphemers far worse than the Saracens, not far away from us but in our midst, so freely and audaciously blaspheme, abuse, and trample on Christ and the Christian sacraments with impunity? (Chazan, *Medieval Stereotypes*, 67.)

By the end of the twelfth century, the accusation that Jews abducted, abused, and crucified Christian children at Easter to parody the Passion of Christ had emerged and begun to claim a place in the anti-Jewish imaginary of many Christians. In some cases, the accusations led to the establishment of lasting saintly cults in religious establishments in England and in Paris. Beyond Thomas of Monmouth's life of William of Norwich, the hagiographies and narratives of twelfth-century child murder "martyrs" have not survived. This lacuna greatly hampers our ability to understand the development of the child murder libel by being able to compare texts. In spite of this, the main elements of the narrative appear clear: the Jews deliberately kidnap a male Christian child around Eastertime, he is gruesomely tortured in a parody of Christ's Passion, put to death by crucifixion, his body is discovered and re-interred, after which the boy-martyr rewards those venerating him by performing miracles. Whether in Norwich, Gloucester, Bury St. Edmunds, or Paris, official support for the cults of children "martyred" by Jews was usually the result of a specific and favourable local context. Some accusations and rumours, deprived of such support, doubtless faded away and went unrecorded.

Before 1200, the child murder libel seems to have remained confined to England and France. It does not appear to have spread to the Holy Roman Empire, Italy, or the Iberian Peninsula. Even if churchmen or laymen were aware of them, this did not result in documented accusations in those parts of Christendom. The frequently repeated claim in Anglophone scholarly works that the Jews of Zaragoza in the Spanish kingdom of Aragón were accused of murdering a Christian child in 1182 is the result of historians picking up and repeating an error made in nineteenth-century antisemitic propaganda.[9] Furthermore, the child murder libel did not enter into the anti-Jewish discourse of twelfth-century Christian polemics. This state of affairs would change in the thirteenth century. Not only would the child murder libel spread to the Empire and the Iberian Peninsula but the libel itself would evolve: alongside the child crucifixion narrative would appear a new and terrifying narrative involving the accusation that Jews consumed the blood of Christian children.

9 François Soyer, "How a Factual Error became a Historical Fact: The 1182 'Ritual Murder' in Zaragoza in Antisemitic Propaganda and Modern Scholarship," *Cadernos de estudos Sefarditas* 24 (2022–2023): 31–57.

Chapter 2

The Birth of the "Blood Libel" and the Thirteenth-Century Papal Reaction

The child murder libel does not appear to have affected Jews in the German-speaking lands of the Holy Roman Empire in the twelfth century, despite the periodic outbreak of anti-Jewish violence. Jewish sources mention a spate of instances before 1200 in which the accusation that Jews had murdered a Christian was a trigger for anti-Jewish riots and massacres, often in the context of the passage of crusaders on their way to the Holy Land. Some accusations involved adult victims and others children, but none involved alleged crucifixions. The case that comes closest to being comparable to those in England or France occurred in the Bavarian town of Würzburg in 1147. A Christian source and a Jewish one both confirm that the Jewish community of Würzburg was attacked after the discovery of the body of a Christian man in the River Main, at the time when crusaders were gathering for the Second Crusade. The sources concord that the mob treated the body as that of a "martyr" and "saint" and accused the Jews of his murder, but both are also clear that it was that of an adult Christian, and they make no mention of any alleged ritual crucifixion (O'Brien, 126–35).

It is in the town of Fulda, in central Germany, that the child murder libel developed into a new, terrifying form in 1235. Our earliest sources for the events themselves are two monastic annals: the *Annales Erphordenses Fratrum Praedicatorum* (Dominican Annals of Erfurt) and the *Annales Marbacenses* from the Augustinian abbey of Marbach in Alsace.

Both sources offer only very brief accounts of the events at Fulda. According to the *Annales Erphordenses*, the Jews of Fulda were accused of murdering the five sons of a Christian miller. The mill was located outside of Fulda and the murders occurred whilst their parents were at church in the town. These annals claim that two Jews killed the boys and "collected their blood in bags smeared with wax" before setting fire to the mill, presumably to conceal their crime. The *Annales Marbacenses* further add that "the Jews killed some Christian boys in a mill-house at the monastery of Fulda so that they might draw out blood from them to heal themselves." The deaths did not occur around Easter but rather, according to the *Annales Erphordenses*, on Christmas Day. The consequences for the Jews of Fulda were dire. Both annals agree that a large number of Jews were killed. The *Annales Marbacenses* merely states that "the citizens of the same city killed many of the Jews," suggesting a violent riot, but the *Annales Erphordenses* indicates that some form of judicial process followed by executions may have taken place. The *Annales Erphordenses* relates the execution of thirty-four Jews of both sexes who were forced to confess.[1] The two annals thus provide only a very brief account of an event that differed markedly from those that had taken place in England or France before 1200. There is no reference to either Easter or the parodying of the Passion and crucifixion of Christ. Instead, the alleged motivation is the collection of blood from Christian children so that it could be used in the production of remedies.

News of the deaths in Fulda spread beyond Fulda and its region and threatened to motivate attacks on Jewish communities elsewhere in the Holy Roman Empire. Indeed, the

---

1 *Annales Erphordenses fratrum praedicatorum*, in *Monumenta Erphesfurtensia saec. XII. XIII. IV.*, edited by Oswald Holder-Egger, Monumenta Germaniae Historica: Scriptores rerum Germanicarum in usum scholarum separatim editi (MGH SS rer. Germ.) 42 (Hannover: Hahn, 1899), 92; *Annales Marbacenses*, edited by Hermann Bloch, MGH SS rer. Germ. 9 (Hannover: Hahn, 1907), 98.

Annales Marbacenses adds that the bodies of the children were transported over two hundred kilometres to the castle of Hagenau and buried there, indicating the possible beginning of a popular saintly cult. Circulating by word of mouth, the news of the events in Fulda and the accusations against the Jews led to quite distorted accounts and rumours. Writing between 1254 and 1265, the monk Richer of Senones reports the murder of three young boys by Jews, wrongly placing the deaths in Hagenau itself. He does not mention the collection blood and, instead of Christmas, he charges the Jews of committing murders during Jewish celebrations of "their Easter" (i.e., Passover) that coincided with the Christian Easter. Moreover, he notes that the boys died when the Jews "used them as playthings in their houses" ("de ipsis quedam ludibria in domibus suis egerunt") suggesting an accusation of ritual crucifixion rather than a new development.[2]

The Holy Roman Emperor, Frederick II, was sufficiently alarmed by "the tumult that had arisen against the Jews at the time" and the risk of a breakdown in law and order that he resolved to hold an official inquiry. The inquiry gathered several Jewish converts to Christianity to examine the charges and, the following year, resulted in the promulgation of an official *Privilege and Sentence in Favour of the Jews*. The text of the 1236 document is illuminating as it offers a clearer account of the nature of "grave crime imputed to the Jews of Fulda" than the two aforementioned annals. The experts gathered by Emperor Frederick were asked to use "their knowledge of Judaism and Jewish books and the Old Testament" and consider "if there survives any belief leading to the perpetrating of any [criminal] act involving human blood, which could have induced the Jews to commit the aforesaid crime." The Emperor's decree states that the unnamed experts utterly rejected the accusation against the Jews. Pointing to Jewish writings and Kosher laws, the experts noted that Jews "guard

2 *Richeri Gesta Senoniensis Ecclesiae*, edited by Georg Waitz et al. MGH: Scriptores 25 (Hanover: Impensis Bibliopolii Hahniani, 1880), 324.

against the intake of all blood" and "for those to whom even the blood of animals is forbidden, the desire for human blood cannot exist, as a result of the horror of the matter, the prohibition of nature and the common bond that ties the human species in which they sit alongside Christians." The decree of Emperor Frederick II absolved the Jews of the accusation and ordered his Christian subjects not to spread it.[3]

The conclusions of the experts reported in the 1236 decree clearly indicate that the accusation against the Jews involved the supposed consumption of human blood. Nevertheless, the decree does not explicitly state whether this accusation involved human blood being used as a medicinal remedy or as food (cannibalism). Based on the evidence, the former seems far more likely than the latter. It is difficult to believe that the accusation of Fulda emerged out of a vacuum. Indeed, ideas about the magical properties of human blood in folklore and the association in the Christian mind of Jews with the practice of magic were seemingly common in the medieval Holy Roman Empire. By way of illustration, *The Song of the Nibelungs* (*Nibelungenlied*), an epic poem written in Middle High German around 1200, features the consumption of human blood and hearts as a way in which to gain bodily strength.

The emergence of the blood libel coincided with a period of change in the attitudes of Christian polemicists towards Jews. The newly created Mendicant Orders—the Dominicans and Franciscans—resulted in a surge of interest in the active evangelization of Jews living in Christendom in the early thirteenth century. Christian polemicists examined Jewish writings with a hostile eye. The Franciscan Nicholas Donin, a former Jew expelled from the Jewish community in Paris, presented a list of thirty-five accusations against the Talmud to Pope Gregory IX in 1236. For Donin, the blasphemous Talmud contained "wicked and abusive things" against Christianity.

3 *Constitutiones et acta publica imperatorum et regum. Tomvs II. inde ab a. MCXCVIII usque ad a. MCCLXXII (1198-1272)*, edited by Ludwig Weiland, MGH: Const. 2 (Hannover: Hahn, 1896), 274–76.

Donin's arguments persuaded the pope to order all Christian princes to confiscate copies of the Talmud in early 1240. In France, the only kingdom to implement the decree, the Crown ordered the burning of twenty-four cartloads of copies of the Talmud in Paris in 1242. For Donin, Judaism was also an existential threat to all Christians. During the infamous disputation between Donin and four French rabbis in Paris in 1240, the convert went as far as to claim that a Talmudic dictum ("the best of Gentiles is to be killed") permitted and encouraged the murder of Gentiles. Ignoring the fact that the dictum applied to the book of Exodus and the Egyptian persecution, Donin gave it a specifically anti-Christian meaning by substituting the word "Christians" for "Gentiles" (*optimum Christianorum occide*).[4]

A little over a decade after the events at Fulda, the accusation that Jews murdered Christian children for their blood resurfaced, this time in Valréas in Provence. Insofar as is known, this case was the first to merge the two dominant narrative elements in the child murder libel: the collection of blood and crucifixion. The Jews of Valréas were accused of murdering a child: unusually not a boy but a girl. The accusation led to the arrest, torture, and gruesome executions of various Jewish men and women as well as the expulsion of others, the seizure of Jewish property and conversion of Jewish children. Crucially, the surviving records of the investigation have survived.[5] They reveal that the body of a two-year-old girl named Meilla was found on March 26, 1247. Three Jews named Bendig, Burcellas, and Durand were arrested for the murder and their confessions were extracted under torture. The authorities consequently arrested other Jewish men and women who were, in turn, tortured and forced to confess. The

4 *The Trial of the Talmud*, ed. John Friedman, Jean Connell Hoff, and Robert Chazan (Toronto: Pontifical Institute of Mediaeval Studies, 2012), 108–9.

5 Auguste Molinier, *Enquête sur un meurtre imputé aux juifs de Valreás* (Paris: Champion, 1883).

recorded confessions of the first three men, extracted under torture and doubtless answering leading questions, involved the collection of blood but they gave different reasons for its alleged use. Bendig stated that a glass recipient was used and that the Jews "had to partake of the said blood on the holy Sabbath just past, and they believed that they would be saved" ("quo de dicto Sanguine debebant communicare die sabbati sancto nuper preterito, et credebant salvari"). Burcellas and Durand, for their part, maintained that the Jews of Valréas had sacrificed the girl in accordance with an ancient Jewish ritual that took place in front of the Temple of Jerusalem. Asked what he intended to do with the blood, Burcellas "said that in ancient times their high priest used to take the blood of a bull, and in the courtyard that was in front of the Temple, which was called Isbea, the blood was sprinkled for the sake of vengeance, according to what is found in the law of Moses." This was apparently a reference to the *mizbeach* (Hebrew: מִזְבֵּחַ: "a place of slaughter or sacrifice") at the Temple in Jerusalem. The tortured prisoners added that after collecting the child's blood, they crucified her on Good Friday as an "insult" (*contumeliam*) to Jesus Christ whom they blamed for their exile from the Holy Land. The men implicated their entire community, but Bendig went further. Indeed, in a story reminiscent of the one recounted by Thomas of Monmouth a century before, he presented the murder as part of a wider Jewish conspiracy to kill Christian children, with its centre in Spain. Bendig also said the same thing, namely "that it is a custom among the Jews, and wherever there is a large population of Jews, to do it by consent, and especially in parts of Spain, because you have the greatest number of Jews, and when they cannot have a Christian, they buy a Muslim."

The child murder libel of Valréas is unique not only because it offers us the first account of a child murder libel sourced from judicial sources but also because it witnessed the first active intervention of the papacy in the child murder libel. The Jews of Provence appealed to the pope for protection. Pope Innocent IV, who was then residing to the north in the town of Lyon, sent a letter to the archbishop of Vienne in

May 1247 in which he noted the discovery in a ditch of the body of a young girl and the accusation that the Jews had crucified her but makes no mention of the accusation that her blood was collected. Pope Innocent deplored the judicial abuses of the local secular authorities and forced conversions of Jewish children. He ordered the archbishop to ensure that "in the future you do not allow Jews to be molested by anyone without cause in these or similar matters."[6]

It may well be that other unrecorded cases or rumours of child murder libel occurred in the German speaking lands of the Holy Roman Empire around this time. Jewish communities there were sufficiently alarmed to seek the help of the papacy. On July 5, 1247, Pope Innocent IV sent an encyclical letter (*Lachrymabilem Judæorum Alemannie*) to the bishops of France and Germany. His condemnation of the idea that Jews killed Christian children "in their religious rites" was unambiguous:

> We have received a mournful complaint from the Jews of Germany, telling how some princes, both ecclesiastical and lay, together with other nobles and powerful persons in your cities and dioceses, devise evil plans against them and invent various pretexts in order to rob them unjustly of their goods, and gain possession thereof. This they do without stopping to consider prudently that it is from the archives of the Jews, so to speak, that the testimonies of the Christian faith came forth. Holy Scripture pronounces among other injunctions of the Law "thou shalt not kill," forbidding them when they celebrate the Passover even to touch any dead body. Nevertheless, they are falsely accused that, in that same solemnity, they make communion with the heart of a slain child. This is alleged to be enjoined by the Law, whereas in fact such an act is manifestly contrary to it. Moreover, if the body of a dead man is by chance found anywhere, they maliciously ascribe the cause of death to the action of the Jews. On this, and many other fictitious pretexts, they rage against the Jews and despoil them of their possessions, against God and Justice and the privileges mercifully granted to them by

6 Elie Berger, *Les registres d'Innocent IV* (Paris: Thorin, 1884), 1:424.

> the Holy See; notwithstanding that they have never been tried for these crimes and have never confessed them and have never been convicted of them. By starvation, imprisonment and many heavy persecutions and oppressions they harass them, inflicting upon them divers kinds of punishment, and condemning large numbers to a most shameful death. Hence the Jews, who are under the power of the aforesaid nobles, lords and princes, are in a worse condition than were their forefathers in Egypt, and are compelled to go into exile from localities where they and their ancestors have dwelt from time immemorial. Wherefore, fearing that they would be utterly exterminated, they have thought well to have recourse to the wisdom of the Apostolic See. We, therefore, being unwilling that the aforesaid Jews should be unjustly harassed (seeing that the compassionate God expects their conversion, and that we believe, according to the testimony of the prophet, that the remnant of them shall be saved), do ordain that you show yourselves favourable and benign towards them. Duly redress all that has been wrought against the Jews in the aforesaid matter by the said prelates, nobles and potentates; and do not allow them in future to be unjustly molested by anybody on this or any other similar charge (Roth, 97–98).

Once more, Innocent does not mention the alleged use of blood. Instead, the accusation condemned is the claim that Jews "make communion with the heart of a slain child." It is not clear whether this is a reference to an accusation that the Jews parodied the Christian communion by eating the heart of a child or whether "communion" here refers to a purported Jewish religious rite.

The first clear papal reference to the accusation that Jews consumed Christian blood came in another document produced in July 1247 when Innocent re-issued the bull *Sicut Iudaeis*. The bull, periodically issued by popes from the twelfth century onward, threatened excommunication against Christians who physically attacked Jews, sought to force them to convert, damaged, or stole their property, and interfered with their religious rites. Innocent's version contains a clear reference to the earlier events at Fulda and the consumption of blood although once again it is not clear whether this supposed consumption was in the form of food or magical remedies:

> Nor shall anyone accuse them [the Jews] of using human blood in their religious rites, since in the Old Testament they are instructed not to use blood of any kind, let alone human blood. But since at Fulda and in several other places many Jews were killed on the grounds of such a suspicion, we strictly forbid that this should be repeated in future. If anyone knowing the tenor of this decree should, God forbid, dare to oppose it, he shall be punished by loss of his rank and office, or be placed under a sentence of excommunication, unless he makes proper amends for his presumption.[7]

Innocent's successor Gregory X was even more explicit in his 1272 version of *Sicut Iudaeis*, warning those Christians who are "envious of the Jews, [some of whom] even hide their children in order to have a pretext to molest the Jews, and to extort money from them so as to pay their dues" against falsely accusing Jews of "killing a Christian child in order to use its heart and blood for sacrifice. This is false and ought not to be believed." Gregory forbade Christians "to make any allegations against the Jews on such a pretext. We command, moreover, that the Jews imprisoned on this account shall be released from prison, and that they shall not be arrested again on such a groundless charge unless (which we think impossible) they are captured *in flagrante delicto*."

Despite such clear papal condemnations, the belief that Jews engaged in acts of ritual cannibalism endured. The Dominican Thomas of Cantimpré (1201–1272) recorded in a compilation of exemplary moral stories a story told to him by two fellow Dominicans of an unnamed seven-year-old girl sold to the Jews by an old Christian woman in the 1260s in Pforzheim (southwestern Germany). According to the story, the Jews "gagged and beat the girl, cut her with knives,

---

7 M. Stern, *Die päpstlichen Bullen über die Blutbeschuldigung* (Munich: Schupp, 1900), 14–17 and 18–22 for quotations below.

expressed her blood, and collected it on cloths." The fantastic story ends with the guilt of the Jews being miraculously exposed after the discovery of the body: when the Jews are marched past the dead body, its wounds immediately gush blood in accusation and the Jews are put to death. Thomas is not explicit about the alleged use that the Jews have for the blood but in a following chapter, entitled "Why does the Jew shed Christian blood every year?," he expands on the topic. He presents the shedding of Christian blood as a regular Jewish "custom" that occurs "in every province in which they live. In fact, certainly it has been adequately demonstrated that they cast lots each year in every province for which city or town will deliver Christian blood to the other cities." Thomas explains this conspiracy in near mystical terms, arguing that Jews were subject to "a stain of blood" (*maculam sanguinis*) after they had told Pilate to crucify Jesus and cried out "His blood be upon us and upon our children" (Matthew 27:25). This regular "flow of blood"—i.e., Jewish male menstruation—could only be cured through the application of "Christian blood alone." Thus, Thomas concludes, "the blind and impious Jews, always seizing upon this remark, began spilling Christian blood each year in every province, so that they might convalesce with such blood." A Jewish source, the Nuremberg *Memorbuch*, confirms the martyrdom of various Jews in Pforzheim in 1267 without specifying the circumstances of their deaths.[8]

The affair at Pforzheim was not an isolated incident. The claim that Jews used Christian blood for therapeutic reasons, especially the "curse" of male menstruation linked to their collective responsibility for the crucifixion of Christ, was firmly established by the fourteenth-century. The early fourteenth-century Dominican Rudolph of Schlettstadt, for example, claimed to have "heard from Jews that certain Jews

---

8 Thomas of Cantimpré, *Bonum universale de apibus* (Douai: Baltazaris Belleri, 1627), 303–5; Isaac ben Samuel and Siegmund Salfeld, *Das martyrologium des Nürnberger Memorbuches* (Berlin: Simion, 1898), 128–29.

descended from those who cried out before Pilate at the time of Christ's passion 'his blood be upon us and on our children' flow every month with blood and often suffer dysentery (from which they frequently die). However, they [believe that they] are healed by the blood of a Christian who has been baptized in the name of Christ" (Resnick, 261). Accusations continued to appear from the thirteenth to the fifteenth centuries in the Holy Roman Empire, the kingdom of Hungary and Switzerland/Savoy. Sometimes, such as at Weissenburg in 1270 or Munich in 1285, our sources are early modern chronicles and thus written centuries later.[9] Three Jewish brothers arrested at Endingen in 1470 for the alleged murder of a family of Christian beggars—parents and their two children—in 1462 confessed under torture to seeking Christian blood for medicinal purposes. For this, the local authorities burned the Jewish brothers at the stake. Similar claims targeted other Jewish communities in the 1460s but on those occasions the Holy Roman Emperor intervened to protect his Jewish subjects (and the fiscal revenue he derived from them) (Po-chia Hsia, *Myth of Ritual Murder*, 14–41).

Whilst the blood libel initially appears to have focused on the alleged use of Christian blood for medicinal purposes, in some cases it involved the claim that Jews ate Christian blood (and sometimes flesh) during the Passover festival. In the Western Alps, judges in Savoy conducted an inquiry after "a substantial public outcry and rumour" accused local Jews of kidnapping and murdering various boys who had disappeared and of "concocting from their heads and intestines a cake or meal, which is called *Aharace*." This, the rumour alleged, was "to be given as food to all the Jews and the said Jews eat of the said food as a sort of substitute Passover festival." In this case, the reference is to *kharóset* (חֲרֹוסֶת), a paste made of fruits and nuts that is one of the symbolic foods eaten at the

9 Bernhard Hertzog, *Chronicon Alsatiae: Edelsasser Cronick* (Strasbourg, Jobin, 1592), 198–201; Johannes Aventinus, *Annalium Boiorum libri VII* (Ingolstadt: Alexander et Samuel Weissenhorn, 1554), 784.

Passover Seder.[10] The same accusation of ritual cannibalism surfaced again at Trent in 1475 (see the next chapter) and in Regensburg in 1476, where six Jews were tortured into confessing that they had killed Christian children to smear their blood on unleavened bread during the Passover festival as well as for magical purposes (Po-chia Hsia, *Myth of Ritual Murder*, 43–85).

The blood libel did not replace the original notion that Jews crucified Christian children. Indeed, that narrative continued to flourish in England. The chronicler Matthew Paris (1200–1259) recorded a spate of instances in which Jews in England were accused of murdering or attempting to murder Christian children to parody the Passion of Christ. In 1240, a Christian man accused the Jews of Norwich of the "extraordinary crime" of circumcising his son and keeping him as a prisoner in order "to crucify him." The father's accusation resulted in the execution of four Jews. In addition to this, Matthew Paris also relates that the discovery of the unburied body of a boy in London in 1244 resulted in a similar accusation as a crowd gathered to examine the corpse. According to Paris, members of the crowd argued that wounds on the boy's body were shaped like Hebrew script, and they dragged Jewish converts to Christianity to the cemetery to confirm this. Initially the converts proclaimed not to recognize any Hebrew letters but, under the pressure of the crowd, changed their minds and stated that they could read the child's name and "words to the effect that he had been sold to the Jews" by unknown persons. Paris records that many Jews fled London in fear of a massacre and the crowd "discovered that the Jews had sometimes perpetrated such crimes, and that the holy bodies, when crucified, had been received in their churches, and had also become renowned by miracles." In the end, however, no violence broke out even though the body was buried in Saint Paul's cathedral (O'Brien, 309–12).

---

10 M. Esposito, "Un procès contre les juifs de la Savoie en 1329," *Revue d'histoire ecclésiastique* 34 (1938): 785–800.

Of all the child murder libels that Matthew Paris records, the most striking and detailed account is that of "Little Saint Hugh" in 1255. Other contemporary Christian sources, the Annals of Waverley and the Annals of Burton, provide accounts that vary in some details but are broadly similar. The accusation followed the by now familiar pattern. The Jews of the cathedral town of Lincoln were accused of kidnapping a boy aged eight or nine named Hugh. According to Matthew Paris, Hugh was last seen "playing with some Jewish boys of his age." The Jews, Paris asserts, abducted the boy and conducted a parody of the trial of Christ by Pilate during which the boy was verbally and physically abused, a crown of thorns was placed on his head, he was crucified and, finally, killed with a lance. After his death, the Jews allegedly disposed of his body in a well because the body miraculously kept re-emerging from the secret grave dug for it. After the discovery of the body, a Jew named Jopin (or Copin), who is presented by Matthew Paris and the Burton Annals as a leading figure of the Jewish community in Lincoln, was accused of orchestrating the murder. An influential nobleman and royal official named John of Lexington took control of proceedings and pressured Jopin into confessing in exchange for a promise to save his life. In total, ninety-one Jews were imprisoned in London and nineteen were executed by order of King Henry III of England, including Jopin.[11]

The child murder narrative of Lincoln follows the classic pattern of disappearance, martyrdom, the discovery of the body and burial in the local cathedral, where the "child-martyr" is venerated and performs miracles. The death of the child is presented both as a ritualized killing motivated by anti-Christian hatred and one that implicates not just one Jew or a Jewish community but all Jews. Matthew Paris's account seems to draw on oral accounts of the events in Lincoln. The words that Paris puts in the mouth of John of Lexington

11 Gavin I. Langmuir, "The Knight's Tale of Young Hugh of Lincoln," *Speculum* 47, no. 3 (1972): 459–82.

indicate that rumours accusing Jews of child murders were pervasive. Indeed, the royal official supposedly told the crowd that "we have already learned that the Jews have not hesitated to attempt such proceedings as a reproach and taunt to our Lord Jesus Christ, who was crucified." Paris also reported that Jopin was coerced into confessing that "what the Christians say is true: for almost every year the Jews crucify a boy as an insult to the name of Jesus. But one is not found every year, for they only carry on these proceedings privately, and in out of the way places." The words that Paris puts into the repentant Jopin's mouth are explicit about the Jews' collective guilt: "I will tell you the truth. Almost all the Jews of England agreed to the murder of this boy." One macabre addition to the traditional narrative is Paris' claim that the Jews disembowelled the corpse of the child "for what reason we do not know, but it was asserted to be for the purpose of practising magical operations." This association of Jews, child murder and black magic had not featured in twelfth-century accusations in England (O'Brien, 314–16).

From the second half of the thirteenth century onwards, the child murder libel incorporated a considerable variety of different narrative elements that sometimes overlapped. The motives ascribed to the Jews extended from the ritual parodying of the crucifixion of Christ to the use of blood for medicinal or magical purposes and even the consumption of Christian blood as a part of the Passover festival. Some chronicles noted accusations incidentally, without much detail. A monk in Colmar, for instance, briefly recorded that in November 1283 "in the area of Mainz a wet nurse sold the male child of a certain knight to the Jews, so that they might kill him and, because of this, the wet nurse and many Jews were shamefully killed by the Christians."[12] The accusation that Jews used murder to obtain Christian blood is known to have occurred on at least twenty-one occasions between 1235 and 1459

12 *Annales aevi Suevici*, edited by Georgius Heinricus Pertz, MGH: Scriptores 17 (Leipzig: Hiersemann, 1925), 210.

(O'Brien, 192–225). In some cases, the different narratives became mixed up in the popular imagination. The discovery of the body of a teenage boy named Werner in 1287 near the Rhineland town of Bacharach led to accusations that the Jews had secretly killed him and the massacre of many Jews in the area. The surviving sources, however, offer contradictory versions of the alleged motive behind the killing. Some claim that it was a ritual crucifixion but another source states that the Jews had "expressed with great violence, as if in a press" the boy's blood to use it for medicinal purposes ("ab eo sanguinem, quo mederi dicunctur, tamquam in torculari multa violencia expresserunt"). In later centuries, amidst a campaign to have the boy canonized, further details were added to the narrative after the construction of an elaborate Gothic chapel overlooking the Rhine for "the Good Werner."[13] Similarly, an accusation made in Tyrnau in 1494 maintained that the Jews killed an adolescent Christian for his blood and used the blood for medicinal purposes (including as a cure for male menstruation). The fifteenth-century Christian author in the Tyrnau case presented the murder as a collective conspiracy to fulfil a religious ritual adding that it occurred because "of an ancient but secret ordinance by which they are under obligation to shed Christian blood in honour of God in daily sacrifices in one spot or another; they said it happened in this manner that the Tyrnau Jews had been chosen that year."[14]

The notion that Jews secretly assembled to kill Christian children and consume their blood represents the pinnacle of extreme antisemitic discourse. The narrative of ritual crucifixion presented the Jews as pitiless child murderers motivated by religious hatred but the blood libel added an extra dimension to the narrative as it stripped Jews of their humanity.

---

13 "Hermanni Altahensis Annales," in *Annales aevi Suevici*, edited by Georgius Heinricus Pertz, MGH: Scriptores 17 (Hannover: Hahn, 1861), 415.

14 Antonii Bonfinii, *Rerum Ungaricarum decades quatuor cum dimidia* (Basel: ex officina Oporiniana, 1568), 736.

It turned them into demonic monsters comparable to alleged witches, who were similarly accused in the fifteenth century of devouring children "contrary to the tendency of human nature."[15] Sometimes, the narratives of ritual crucifixion and blood consumption became linked as Jews were accused of tormenting and crucifying boys before killing them and collecting their blood. The crucifixion and blood libel narratives were certainly both at the heart of the most notorious of all medieval child murder libels and the case which has come to represent the child murder narrative in the modern popular imagination: the death of "Saint" Simon of Trent in 1475.

15 Christopher S. Mackay, *The Hammer of Witches: A Complete Translation of the Malleus Maleficarum* (Cambridge: Cambridge University Press, 2009), 281.

Chapter 3

Simon of Trent (1475): Apex of the Blood Libel

On March 23, 1475, a Christian toddler named Simon disappeared in the town of Trent in the Trentino-Alto Adige region of alpine northern Italy and remained missing despite a search. Rumours among the Christian population rapidly began to cast suspicion upon the Jews of the town. As part of the wider effort to locate the lost boy, the chief magistrate (*podestà*) Giovanni de Salis conducted a fruitless search of the house of Samuel, one of the heads of the small Jewish community of Trent, which consisted of a mere three households. Three days later, on the evening of Sunday, March 26, a Jewish man named Seligman went to fetch some water from a flowing watercourse in the cellar of Samuel's house in order to fill the Jewish ritual bath (*mikveh*), which was used for the purpose of immersion to achieve ritual purity. Seligman, a servant in the household of his master Samuel, found the body of a small child floating in the water. How the body of the child ended up in the watercourse under Samuel's house remains a mystery: had someone deliberately placed it there or did the flowing water carry the corpse there after the boy accidently drowned?

The Jews of Trent rapidly realized the gravity of the situation. The timing could not have been worse, as the boy had disappeared on Maundy Thursday and his body had appeared in a Jewish house on the evening of Easter Sunday. The Tridentine Jews evidently realized that the conditions were ripe for a child murder accusation. After hurried discussions, they decided to report the grim discovery to the Christian authorities and hope that the latter would protect them. This was a logical move and one that other Jewish communities had previously adopted. In the case of the Jews of Trent, however, this turned out to be a catastrophic error. Far from protecting them, the authorities in Trent would take up the accusation and initiate a wave of trials that ended in the destruction of the Jewish community in Trent and the emergence of a notorious blood libel cult that surpassed all others before it in terms of its fame and impact.

Located in the extreme south of the Holy Roman Empire, Trent was the chief city of the prince-bishopric of Trent. In 1475 it was ruled by a joint secular-ecclesiastic prince: the prince-bishop Johannes Hinderbach. Hinderbach had risen to prominence in the service of Emperor Frederick III, who rewarded him with the position of prince-bishop of Trent. The prince-bishop's attitude towards Jews before the events in Trent during the 1470s is a mystery. He is not known to have authored any anti-Jewish pamphlets, sermons, or diatribes. Nevertheless, in view of his subsequent actions, it seems reasonable to assume as the historian Ronnie Po-Chia Hsia has done, that he "was very much shaped by a culture and a historical era, which castigated Jews as the quintessential internal enemies of Christians" (Po-chia Hsia, *Trent 1475*, 13). As Bishop of Trent, Johannes Hinderbach came to play a leading role in the emergence of the cult of the boy who would eventually become widely known as "little saint Simon" (San Simonino).

Instead of seeking to hush-up the discovery of the body in a Jewish house in order to protect the Jews, the authorities in Trent arrested many of them, including the heads of the three households. They imprisoned them in the fortress dominating the town and a full legal investigation began. The surviving evidence is clear that the *podestà* and his officials applied torture and used leading questions as the Jews were interrogated one after another. The *podestà* Giovanni de Salis' investigation followed a pre-determined assumption that the murder was a case of religiously motivated child murder. Coincidentally, the Christian authorities had also imprisoned a Jewish convert to Christianity named Giovanni da Feltre in the castle for an ordinary crime and the *podestà* questioned him "to get information [about] whether or not it is true that Jews are used to killing Christian boys and taking their blood, as it is reported." The surviving record of the interrogation of Giovanni da Feltre is in Latin and the precise wording and language of the questions put to him is unclear. Giovanni recalled a story, probably recounted to him by his father, of a blood libel accusation targeting the Jewish community of Landshut in Bavaria in 1440. The Jews had been accused of killing a child "to get his blood ... but it is not clear how the child was killed or by whom" (Teter, 50). When he was asked whether he had ever witnessed Jews use blood, the Latin summary suggests that Giovanni, who was initially hesitant, told his interrogators about a custom during the Passover Seder in German-speaking Jewish circles, during which participants remove a drop of wine from their cup using their fingertip at the mention of each of the ten plagues, the first one of which of course involved the turning of water into blood. Giovanni stated that his father had filled the cup with blood instead of wine and added the claim that the ceremony involved the cursing of the Christian faith. Finally, he claimed that blood was used to make the unleavened Passover Bread although he stated that he did not know how. The context in which these claims were made—what was the exact wording of the questions and responses in their original language? Was pressure placed upon Giovanni da Feltre? Did he fear for his safety or even his life?—is not known. The *podestà* unquestioningly used Giovanni da Feltre's testimony and the assumption that a child murder had been committed to collect Christian blood as the starting point for his interrogations of the Jews of Trent.

The narrative of Simon's "martyrdom" at the hands of the Jews took form even before the official investigation had ended. On April 4, 1475, just over a week after the discovery of the body, Bishop Hinderbach's physician Giovanni Mattia Tiberino wrote an account of the affair and dispatched it to the senate of the town of Brescia (a town located to the southwest of Trent). A printed version soon appeared with the prolix Latin title *Passio beati Simonis pueri Tridentini a p[er] fidis Iudeis nup[er] occisi; qua[m] Iohannes Mathias Tiberini liberaliu[m] artiu[m] & medici[n]e doctor ad rectores & ciues Brixienses succincte scripsit* (The Passion of the blessed Simon, the boy of Trent, who had just been killed by the perfidious Jews, which Giovanni Mattia Tiberino, a liberal artist and medical doctor, wrote succinctly to the governors and citizens of Brescia). Tiberino had close links with both the bishop and the *podestà* and was one of the medical practitioners who conducted an autopsy of Simon's body. At this point, no Jew had yet confessed but Tiberino's narrative offered a coherent blood libel narrative. Tiberino grandiloquently introduced the story of Simon as "a most important event, such as no era—from the Lord's Passion up to these times—has ever heard of." His stated objective is to ensure that the Jews who "devour our sons, afflicting them with terrible punishment in their synagogues, and cruelly slaughtering them in place of Christ" should "be eliminated from the whole Christian world" and consigned to infamy (Teter, 47–49).

The narrative crafted by Tiberino follows many tropes that were classic in saintly martyrdom narratives (*passiones*) and most of the elements of the anti-Jewish child murder libels. He begins by describing a conspiratorial gathering of the Jews of Trent in a synagogue during the Christian Holy Week before Easter in which the Jews plot the death of a Christian child. Tiberino fashioned a dialogue between the Jews in which they expressed their need to kill a Christian child in order to use its "gore" in their unleavened bread. The reason for the plot is partly medicinal as Tiberino explains that the Jews do this to cure "the powerful stench they exude." Young Simon is depicted as saintly both in terms of his beauty and character whilst the Jews are dehumanized to the extent that they become animalistic. Samuel is "like a tiger eager for blood," while the other Jews "howled for Christian blood" when Simon is led into their presence in Samuel's house. Tiberino describes the torture and death of the gagged Simon in horrifically graphic, even grotesque, detail. The Jews fall upon the boy and tear pieces of his flesh with pincers, they circumcise his penis and collect blood from the wounds. Finally, the Jews stab his body with needles and crucify the moribund boy. As if the description were not clear enough, Tiberino has the Jews utter a chant rendered in pseudo-Hebrew (presumably to add verisimilitude to his narrative) which he translates for his audience as follows: "Let us butcher this boy just like Jesus, the Christians' God, who is nothing. Thus may our enemies be eternally confounded." Tiberino spelled out the conclusion that he wanted his listeners and readers to reach: the "cruel Jews" were a danger to the safety of all Christians and only the expulsion "of this savage race from the whole Christian world" would ensure the safety of Christian children. Furthermore, in what may have been either a rhetorical flourish or a call for the wholesale slaughter of all Jews, Tiberino wishes that "the remembrance of them [would] utterly vanish from the land of the living." The following year, a complete hagiographical history of the boy (*Historia completa de passione et obitu pueris Simonis*) followed the printed version of Tiberino's address to the Brescian senate.

Tiberino's early account of the death of Simon indicates that the Christian population and authorities in Trent had already embraced the notion that it was a child murder committed by Jews for religious purposes. It was with this presupposition that the investigations began. The Jewish prisoners initially resisted attempts to incriminate them in the death of Simon. Instead, they maintained that the Jews of Trent were being framed for the death of the boy. Soon, however, relentless questioning and torture began to mould the answers of the desperate prisoners and secure confessions (although these were still often contradictory). The pressure is evident in the interrogation records. One of the Jewish prisoners asked his interrogator on April 13, 1475: "what should I say?" Similarly Lazarus, a Jew who had the misfortunate to be travelling through Trent when the body of Simon was discovered and was caught up in the investigations, pleaded to his tormentors: "tell me what you want me to say and I will say it." Despite an intervention by the Duke of Tyrol, Trent's overlord, the trials continued and resulted in the execution in June 1475 of seven Jewish men as well as the posthumous "execution" of one who had been found dead in his cell. Other Jews remained on trial and, by then, the papal curia in Rome had decided to intervene.

Hundreds of miles to the south, Pope Sixtus IV in Rome regarded developments in Trent with misgivings. A papal envoy, Bishop Battista dei Giudici of Ventimiglia, was dispatched to Trent to investigate the veracity and legality of the accusations against Jews and provide an opinion on the validity of the emerging saintly cult. Giudici arrived in Trent in September 1475 but Bishop Hinderbach and the advocates of Simon's cult obstructed his investigation and worked hard to promote the cult of Simon while discrediting Giudici. Hinderbach prevented Giudici's access to the remaining Jewish prisoners and the trial documents. The papal envoy was eventually forced to relocate to the town of Rovereto, further south, and received copies of the interrogations that appear to have been heavily doctored. Giudici's intervention was a failure, and it certainly did not save the remaining Jews in Trent. Nevertheless, on October 10, 1475, Pope Sixtus issued a letter to all rulers in Italy forbidding the veneration of Simon until Giudici had concluded his investigations. Moreover, the pontiff wrote to Hinderbach to demand the release of the Jewish women and children. Hinderbach and the *podestà* Giovanni de Salis merely ignored these threats (even though Giudici excommunicated Salis). The Jewish women were put on trial and in January 1477 three of them were forced to confess their guilt (and that of their husbands) in the death of Simon before being converted to Christianity in a spectacular public ceremony. Bishop Hinderbach claimed that the Jews had plotted to poison him and to undermine the cult of Simon by stealing the child's corpse and bribing a notary named Paolo de Novara to alter the trial records. Hinderbach and his supporters were eventually able to claim a measure of victory when, on June 20, 1478, Pope Sixtus issued a bull declaring the trial to be legally valid even though the pope stopped short of officially endorsing the cult of Simon or the blood libel. Even before this papal bull was issued, however, news of the events in Trent travelled fast and had begun to spread.

The reason why the story of "little Simon of Trent" resonated across Europe is due to a combination of factors beyond Tiberino's works. Firstly, there is Trent's geographical location. The town was located astride one of the main roads connecting the Italian Peninsula and the German-speaking lands of the Holy Roman Empire to the north of the Alps via the Brenner Pass. Merchants, churchmen, diplomats and pilgrims travelling via the Brenner Pass to Rome or even the Holy Land inevitably stopped in the town to rest and frequently visited the shrine of the child. A Swiss Dominican friar named Felix Fabri (1441–1502) has left an interesting description of his stay in Trent in 1483 during a pilgrimage to the Holy Land:

> In this city, in 1475, the holy child Simon was martyred by the Jews with great torture; wherefore the Jews were condemned to be hanged after suffering great tortures. I myself beheld their accursed bodies on gibbets the next year when I went to Rome. The body of the holy child, when it was found, began to be famous for the miracles which it wrought, and is still said to be famous. Wherefore people from distant parts of Germany, France and Italy make pilgrimages thither, and bring offerings of wax, clothing, gold and silver plate, and money, in such quantities as is wonderful to behold. Because of this, they have pulled down the old church of Saint Peter, in which the body used to be kept, and have built a new and spacious one upon the same site out of these offerings; moreover, they have cleansed the house of the martyr and consecrated it as a church. So when we pilgrims had taken off our riding-dresses, we went to the churches to obtain indulgences, and in the Church of Saint Peter we saw the body of the holy child and the place of his martyrdom, and the old cathedral church, and other chapels and churches.[1]

1 *The Library of the Palestine Pilgrims' Text Society: The Wanderings of Felix Fabri* (vol. 1, part 1), trans. Aubrey Stewart (London: Committee of the Palestine Exploration Fund, 1896), 69–70.

Felix Fabri's description is striking for a number of reasons. Less than a decade after the trial of the Jews of Trent, the cult of Simon was not only successful in terms of the number of pilgrims it attracted but also due to their lucrative donations. Indeed, Fabri suggests that some pilgrims were not merely visiting the body of Simon whilst passing through Trent but travelling to Trent for that expressed purpose. It also reveals the great efforts made by Bishop Hinderbach to develop Trent into a major place of pilgrimage. The following year, the Spanish theologian Jaime Pérez de Valencia referred in passing to the story of Simon of Trent in his commentary on the Psalm, describing it as "a case famous in all of Italy, Germany and France." Interestingly, Jaime Pérez de Valencia notes that the boy was "crucified" but omits to mention the allegation that the Jews had collected the boy's blood.[2]

News of the death of Simon and the cult that it spawned travelled both north and south of the Alps but this transmission did not just happen through manuscript letters or oral accounts. Unlike the earlier medieval child murder libels, the nascent cult of Simon also benefitted from the effects of the first media revolution in late fifteenth-century Europe. The printing press allowed the story of Simon's "martyrdom" at the hands of the Jews to have a wide and far-reaching impact. Accounts of the "martyrdom" in vernacular German began to appear soon after the end of the trial. Tiberino's narrative was rapidly translated into vernacular German by Günther Zainer and printed in 1475, appearing in Augsburg with the title *Die Geschicht und Legend von dem seyligen Kind und Marterer genannt Symon von den Juden zu Trientt gemarteret und getöttet* (The History and Legend of the Blessed Child and Martyr known as Simon, martyred and killed by the Jews of Trent.) The same year, Matthäus Künig composed a long poem dedicated to "Holy Simon" that appeared in print and Albert Kunne's *Hystorie von Simon zu Trient*, printed in Sep-

2 Jaime Pérez de Valencia, *Commentum in psalmos* (Valencia: Alfonsus Fernandez de Corduba et Gabriel Ludovicus de Arinyo, 1484), fol. 190v.

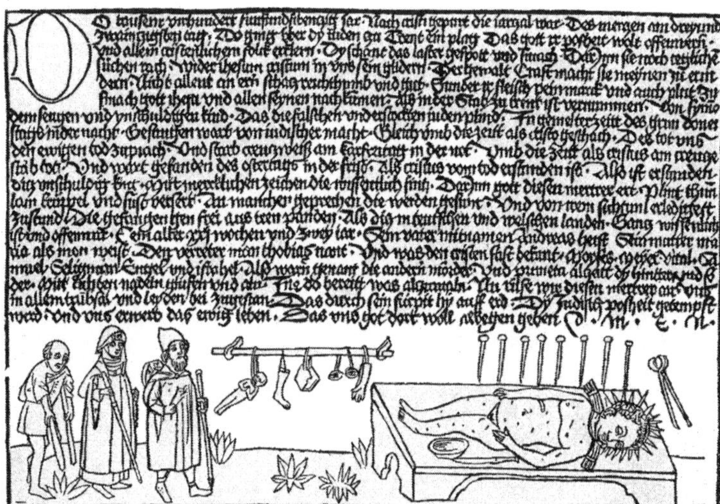

Figure 2. Pilgrims visiting the body of Simon of Trent, laid out and surrounded with the instruments of torture. From an edition of the letter sent by Johannes Matthias to the Senate of Brescia, printed in German by Friedrich Creussner in Nuremberg in 1475. Charles Walker Collection/Alamy Stock Photo. Used with permission.

tember 1475, is another good example. Kunne's work is a short, twenty-eight-page account in German of the death of Simon.

In a European context where the majority of the population remained illiterate, the development of a particular iconography was also a key factor in efforts to disseminate and promote the cult of Simon. Kunne's *Hystorie von Simon zu Trient* not only included a German account of the martyrdom narrative and trial (and execution) of the Jews of Trent but every second page is a crude woodcut illustration designed to accompany the text and reinforce the message of Simon's innocence, his brutal death, his saintly attributes, and the righteous punishment inflicted on the Jews. Early on, the iconography of "Saint" Simon of Trent followed three emotive types, identified by Magda Teter. The first type of image focused on his supposed murder or "martyrdom," depicting the diminutive figure of Simon held by Jews as they bleed him and strangle him with a rope. The second type depicts the deceased Simon's mutilated body, laid out and usually surrounded with the instruments of torture used by his tormentors (see Figure 2). In Frankfurt, people entering and leaving the town through the bridge tower during the early modern period could admire a mural with both a lurid image of the *Judensau*—the portrayal of Jews riding on female pigs, suckling at their udders, and either eating their excrement or kissing the animals' anus—as well as a depiction of Simon's corpse with the tool of his martyrdom and the following caption: "In 1475, on Holy Thursday, the child Simon was two years old when he was killed by the Jews." Finally, a third type appeared depicting the young Simon standing "in glory" or "triumphant," holding a banner and with representations of the instruments of his martyrdom. These three types of iconography would become the dominant ones in the early modern and modern period, copied and repeated in artworks and publications. Their emotive dimension—eliciting compassion for the boys' suffering and hatred of the Jews—doubtless played their part in disseminating the story of Simon.

The dissemination of the story and iconography of Simon of Trent was not just the result of the printing of hagiographical works and pamphlets. As the study of the legend of Saint Simon of Trent and its dissemination by Magda Teter has proved, the narrative of Simon established itself in Christian culture and mentality by means of its inclusion in printed works not "devoted directly to Jews that included stories about them and that were difficult to dismiss." One notable example is the 1493 chronicle of Hartmann Schedel, printed in Nuremberg. Known in English as the *Nuremberg Chronicle* and in German as the *Schedelsche Weltchronik* (Schedel's World History). The work included six hundred and forty-five original woodcut illustrations, and it is one of the best-documented early printed books. It was a commercial success—indeed a best seller for its time—with editions appearing in

German and Latin.[3] The 1493 Latin edition includes a full-page entry on the story of "the blessed Simon of Trent," which offers a concise summary of the story of Simon's "martyrdom" accompanied by a large woodcut illustration of the "martyrdom," possibly crafted by the renowned Renaissance printmaker and artist Albrecht Dürer. Heavily inspired from earlier woodcuts, this horrifying and eye-catching woodcut would have captured the attention of the readers of Schedel's work. It centres on the boy, who is surrounded and grasped by Jews. One Jew is holding up the child while others are stabbing him with needled and collecting his blood in a receptacle at his feet. The Jews each have a small caption with an identifying name (see Figure 3). Later editions changed the format—making the woodcut illustration smaller for example—but the story remained. The inclusion of Simon's story in Schedel's work, albeit in a shortened form, is important because it helped not just to popularize the story but also gave it credibility. Simon's "martyrdom" takes its place in world history and is presented as an averred historical fact, alongside other political and religious events.

The death of Hinderbach in 1486 deprived the emerging cult of Simon of its most powerful supporter but did not end it. His successors in the See of Trent continued to support it, albeit without the original enthusiasm of Hinderbach. Nevertheless, the process through which authoritative hagiographical works whose aim was not primarily antisemitic disseminated the legend of Saint Simon of Trent continued apace. Laurentius Surius (1522–1578), a German Carthusian hagiographer, reproduced Tiberino's narrative of the "most innocent martyr Simon cruelly put to death by the Jews" in his 1571 collection of the lives of the saints.[4] It was primarily

---

3 David Cushing Duniway, "A Study of the Nuremberg Chronicle," *The Papers of the Bibliographical Society of America* 35, no. 1 (1941): 17–34.

4 Laurentius Surius, *De probatis Sanctorum historiis ab Al. Lipomano olim conscriptis nunc primum a Laur. Surio emendatis et auctis*

Das sechst alter

Symon das sellig kindlein zu Trient ist añ.xxi.tag des Mertzen nach der gepurt Cristi.M.cccc.lxxv.iar.in d heiligen martterwochen in der statt Trient von den iuden getödt vnd ein martrer Cristi worden.dann als die iuden in derselben statt wonende ir ostern nach irem sytten begeen wolten vnd doch kein cristenlichs plůt zu geprauch irs vngesewrten prots hetten do brachten sie diss kindlein verstolens in Samuelis eins iuden haws. in solcher gestalt.an dem dritte tag vor ostern vmb versperzeit sasse diss kindlein vor seins vaters thür in abwesen seiner eltern do nehnet sich Thobias ein iüdischer verreter zu disem kindlein das noch nit dreymal zehen monat alt was.dem redet er mit schmaychlenden worte zu vnd trůg es pald in das haws Samuelis. Als nw die nacht herfiele do frewten sich Samuel Thobias Vitalis Moyses Jsrahel vnd Mayer vor der synagog vber vergiessung cristenlichs plůts.Nw entplössßeten sie das kindlein vnd legten ime ein faciletlein vmb sein helsslein das man es nit schreyen hören möcht vnd spanneten ime sein ermlein auss.schnytten ime erstlich sein mälich glidlein ab vnd auss seinem rechten wenglein ein stücklein vnd stachen es allenthalben mit scharpffen spitzigen stacheln heftlein oder nadeln.einer die hend der ander die füsslein haltende.vnd als sie nw das plůt grawsamlich gesamelt hetten do hůben sie an lobsang zesingen vnd zu dem kindlein mit hönischen bedroewortten zesprechen Nym hin du gehangner Jhesu also haben dir ettwen vnsser eltern gethan.also sollen alle cristen in hymel.auff erden vnd meer geschend werden.dieweil verschied das vnschuldig mertrerlein.die iuden eylete zum nachtmal vnd assen von dem plůt das vngesewerte zu schmahe Cristo vnsserm hayland vnd wurffen de tote leichnã in ein fliessends wasser nahent bey irem haws vnnd hielten ir ostern mit frewden.Die bekümerten eltern süchten ir verlorns kindlein.das funden sie vber drey tag in dem fluss.Als solchs an Johanssen von Salis den edeln burger von Brixien kaiserlicher rechten doctor vnd dessmals öbersten pfleger gelanget do hiess er nach den iude greiffen vnd sie mit marter anzichen.also das sie nach ordnung ansagten wie sie dise misstat begangen hetten. vnd darauff warden sie mit gepürlicher straff aussgetilgt.Als der leichnam auff befelhe Johãssen hinderbachs bischoffs daselbst bestattet wardt do fieng er alsspald an in wunderzaichen zescheinen vnd auss allen cristenlichen gegenten zu dises heilliges kindes grab ein zulawff zewerden.dauon dañ dise statt nicht kleine auffung vnnd zunemung empfunden hat.vnd die burger daselbst haben disem leichnam ein schöne kirchen auffgerichtet.

Dergleichen vbeltat haben auch die iuden vber fünff iar darnach in dem stettlein Mota in Foriaul gelegẽ mit ertödtung eins andern kinds begangen.darumb warden der teter drey gefangẽ gein Venedig gefüert vnd nach grawsamer peyn verpreñt.

Die Türcken zohen abereins in nydern Misiam vnd warden mit grosser schlacht ernydergelegt. Darnach eroberten die Genueser die grossen statt Capham die die Türcken noch inhetten.aber dieselb statt kome in disem iar durch verretterey vnd dargebung eins Genuesischen burgers widerumb in der Türcken gewalt.

Figure 3. The death of Simon of Trent. Image from Hartmann Schedel's *Weltchronik* (Nuremberg: Anton Koberger, 1493), fol. 254v. Heritage Image Partnership Ltd./Alamy Stock Photo. Used with permission.

in the 1580s that the narrative and cult of Simon acquired a new credibility from papal recognition. The reform of the liturgical calendar ordered by Pope Gregory XIII led to the inclusion of Simon in the *Martyrologium Romanum* alongside other martyrs officially recognized by the Church in 1583. The *Martyrologium* described Simon as "an innocent boy cruelly killed by the Jews out of hatred of the church, who later accomplished many miracles." Inclusion in the *Martyrologium Romanum* turned Simon's martyrdom into a officially sanctioned historical fact for many of the faithful as the purpose of the reformed calendar was to eliminate those popular saints whose narratives and cults were deemed to lack credibility and tainted by "superstition." Five years later, Pope Sixtus V granted a liturgy (*officium*) in the name of Simon. While this was not an official recognition of Simon's claim to "sainthood," many early modern Catholics perceived it as another endorsement of the cult.

In the seventeenth century, the Bollandist society, an association of scholars, theologians, philologists, and historians devoted to the study of hagiography and the cult of the saints in Christianity included a lengthy entry on the narrative and miracles of *S. Simon a iudaeis necati* (S[aint] Simon killed by the Jews) in their encyclopaedic and influential *Acta Sanctorum* (the lives of Saints), printed in Antwerp. Their principal source of information was, once more, Tiberino's narrative. It is noteworthy that Simon was no longer referred to as just a martyr but as "saint" alongside other saints in the *Acta Sanctorum.* This unofficial elevation of Simon to sainthood would be followed by eighteenth-century authors like the Venetian writer Flaminio Cornaro with his *De cultu Sancti Simonis pueri Tridentini* (Venice, 1753).[5] A measure of the

(Cologne: apud Geruinum Calenium & hæredes Quentelios, 1571), 2:356–59.

5 Daniel van Papenbroeck, Godefridus Henschenius, and Joannes Bollandus, *Acta sanctorum Martii: Tomvs III* (Antwerp: apud Jacobum Meursium, 1668), 494–502.

extent to which Simon of Trent's martyrdom had come to be considered as a historical "fact" within the church hierarchy can be gauged from an internal report written in 1758 by Cardinal Giovanni Ganganelli. The cardinal was tasked with an investigation into the truth of the blood libel, "based on the claim that their famed unleavened bread is adulterated with human blood and especially that of Christians." Ganganelli's final report highlighted the past condemnations of medieval popes and theologians and methodically examined the arguments put forward by proponents of the blood libel, whose authority and credibility he attacked. Ganganelli considered the case of Simon of Trent "who was martyred by the Jews in 1475" and "well known to the world":

> The case of the Blessed Simon of Trent, I must pass on to the consideration of real and established facts. I admit, then, as true the fact of the Blessed Simon, a boy three years old, killed by the Jews in Trent in the year 1475 in hatred of the faith of Jesus Christ (although it is disputed by Basnage and Wagenseil); for the celebrated Flaminio Cornaro, a Venetian senator, in his work *On cult of the child St. Simon of Trent* [Venice, 1753, &c.] disposes of all the doubts raised by the abovementioned critics. It should, however, be noted that Sixtus IV ..., in whose pontificate this tragic event occurred in Trent, promulgated an apostolic brief in which he forbade the devotion which was paid to the aforesaid Blessed Simon by his fellow-citizens. Indeed, the matter went so far that this devotion remained forbidden during the course of nearly a century, until in 1588 the great Pontiff Sixtus V ..., by his apostolic brief, conceded the office and proper Mass in honour of the blessed Simon, adding to these a plenary indulgence to any person who, having confessed and communicated, visited on his feast the church in which his relics are to be found (Roth, 82).

Ganganelli disingenuously categorizes the case of Simon as a murder committed "in hatred of the faith" and not as a "blood accusation," which it certainly was. Clearly, whatever his personal beliefs or scruples about the cult of Simon, Ganganelli did not think that it could be dismissed.

Despite never being canonized or even beatified by the Papacy, "Saint" Simon of Trent and his cult became the epitome of the blood libel in the medieval period and, arguably, even today. This notoriety was not just a result of the place (on the border between Italy and the Holy Roman Empire) and time (with the advent of the printing press) in which it occurred. Its perpetuation into the modern period arose through Simon's inclusion by early modern hagiographers alongside other more "respectable" saints of the Church whose holiness and miracles were deemed credible enough to merit veneration and liturgies. This state of affairs would continue well into the twentieth century, and it is only after the Second Vatican Council (1962–1965) that the cult of Simon was abolished in 1965 and that the "boy martyr" was removed from the official martyrology of the Roman Catholic Church.

Chapter 4

El Santo Niño de la Guardia: The Child Murder Libel in the Iberian Peninsula

A flourishing Jewish population lived in the Christian kingdoms of the medieval Iberian Peninsula, possibly the largest in Western Christendom. Accusations against Jewish communities involving the child murder libel only appeared there towards the end of the thirteenth century. The legend of "Saint" Dominguito de Val, which alleges that the Jews of Zaragoza in the kingdom of Aragon abducted and crucified a seven-year-old boy in 1250, appears to be a later tradition and no thirteenth-century evidence confirming the existence of the boy or the accusation has yet surfaced.[1] There is, admittedly, a clear reference to the child murder libel in the *Siete Partidas*, a legal compendium collated and created during the 1250s and 1260s in the Christian kingdom of Castile under King Alfonso X of Castile:

> We have heard it said that in some places Jews celebrated, and still celebrate Good Friday, which commemorates the Passion of Our Lord Jesus Christ, by way of contempt; stealing children and fastening them to crosses, and making images of wax and crucifying them, when they cannot obtain children; we order that, hereafter, if in any part of our dominions anything like this is done, and can be proved, all persons who were present when the act was committed

1 François Soyer, "From Medieval Ritual Murder to Modern Blood Libel: The Narrative of 'Saint' Dominguito de Val in Spain," *Antisemitism Studies* 5, no. 1 (2021): 139–74.

> shall be seized, arrested and brought before the king; and after the king ascertains that they are guilty, he shall cause them to be put to death in a disgraceful manner, no matter how many there are.[2]

The phrasing of this text, however, is ambiguous. It acknowledged rumours and hearsay ("we have heard it said") that the accusation of the ritual crucifixion of children occurred "in some places." This could suggest an awareness of accusations elsewhere in Europe but does not constitute evidence of actual accusations in the Iberian Peninsula by that point in the thirteenth century. King Alfonso's main aim appears to have been to pre-empt trouble by emphasizing the jurisdiction that the Crown had over the investigation of such accusations against Jews. This was doubtless a wise precaution as stories linking Jews to the deaths of children were certainly circulating in the thirteenth-century Iberian Peninsula. The *Cantigas de Santa Maria*, a collection of over four hundred poems in Galician-Portuguese recounting miracles accomplished by the Virgin Mary that was collated during the reign of the same King Alfonso X of Castile, features the story of the murder of a Christian choirboy in England by a Jew. Although the murder is presented as motivated by religious anger, there is no allegation of a plot organized by the Jewish community or, more crucially, of an attempt to parody the Passion of Christ or to collect the boy's blood for medicinal or even magical purposes. In a polemical work completed in 1278, the Catalan Dominican friar Raymond Martin asserted that "[the Jews'] plan for Christians is this one: to kill Christians, and kill their children by casting them into wells and pits, when they can do this secretly."[3] Martin does not mention any supposedly ritualistic aspect seeking to parody the

2 *Las Siete Partidas*, vol. 5, *Underworlds: The Dead, the Criminal, and the Marginalized* (Philadelphia: University of Pennsylvania Press, 2001), 1434.

3 Jeremy Cohen, *The Friars and the Jews: The Evolution of Medieval Anti-Judaism* (Ithaca: Cornell University Press, 1982), 129–69.

death of Christ but the reference to the specific targeting of Christian children is striking.

The earliest documentary reference to what appears to be an anti-Jewish child murder accusation featuring ritual or magical motives in the Iberian Peninsula only emerges in 1294. In a letter sent by the King of Aragon James II (1291–1327) to his officials in the town of Zaragoza, the king noted rumours circulating that the Jewish community had abducted a Christian boy, "beheaded him and taken the liver and the heart from his body" before secretly burying his corpse. Consequently, the terrified Jewish community of Zaragoza had complained to the King that they "did not dare to appear among those Christians." Nonetheless, the missing child was found safe and sound in the nearby town of Calatayud. An angry James II ordered his officials to severely punish any person who spread such rumours, "as a result of which our *aljama* [Jewish community in Zaragoza] might be destroyed." The fourteenth and early fifteenth centuries offer further evidence of child murder accusations in Barcelona (1301), Mallorca (1309), and Valencia (1330) in which Jews were accused of murdering a child, or feared being accused of such a murder, after the discovery of a child's body. Nevertheless, in all these cases there is not enough evidence to be certain of the nature of the accusation. Particularly interesting is a spate of documents from the Pyrenean kingdom of Navarre that record instances in which accusations of child murder against Jews were linked to the practice of magic. These include a Christian woman arrested in 1332 "for having killed an infant in order to give its heart to the Jews" and a Christian couple executed in 1334 for the "killing a child in order to give its heart and blood to the Jews in exchange for money." These terse references, unfortunately, do not offer further details about the accusation made against the Jews or the ultimate fate of the Jews involved. As such, it is not clear whether the child murder accusation was one that involved black magic, the use of hearts and blood for supposedly medicinal purposes or some other "Jewish ritual" (Soyer, 309–30).

It is only in the middle of the fifteenth century that more detailed information becomes available about a series of accusations that fit the various strands of the anti-Jewish child murder narrative. Christian and Jewish sources record instances in which the child murder narrative targeted Jewish communities in the kingdom of Castile. The Franciscan Alonso de Espina presented three cases supposed to have occurred in Castile in his infamous polemic *Fortalitium fidei*. Espina claims that he was staying in the town of Valladolid in 1454 and, after making it known that he wished to preach a sermon on the cruelty of the Jews, "certain persons worthy of credit" came forward, including García Martínez de Baamonde, the bishop of Lugo, "a man of great knowledge and good conscience" to tell him about an alleged case of child murder by Jews. The story Espina recounts is that two Jews murdered a Christian child in the countryside in the lands of "Don Luis de Almansa" and extracted the child's heart so that the local Jewish community could burn it to ashes, mix it with wine and drink it. When dogs uncovered the child's corpse, the local lord conducted a "careful investigation" into the boy's death and arrested a "red-haired Jew," whom he sent to the jail in Valladolid, before informing the bishop of Lugo. Espina concludes his account by claiming that the Jews used their influence at the royal court to quash the legal proceedings and asserting that they secured the collaboration of judges descended from Jews (*conversos*).[4]

Two early modern Jewish sources record a similar accusation. The first is Samuel Usque, a descendant of Portuguese Jews forced to convert to Christianity in 1497, and the second is Joseph Ha-Cohen (1496–ca. 1577), whose family fled from Navarre to Italy following the expulsion of the Jews from Spain. These Jewish sources, which were based on earlier but lost Jewish accounts, offer a similar story with only a few different details, in which Christian thieves murder the boy in

4 Alonso de Espina, *Fortalitium fidei* (Nuremberg: Anton Koberger, 1494), fol. 146r–v.

order to rob him of some jewellery. The discovery of the body, however, leads the Christian population to accuse the Jews of the crime:

> Everyone was discussing who could have committed such a cruel act. They said that it could not be believed that the culprit could be a Christian since the boy was so innocent and small that he could not have offended anyone. They opined that it must have been a Muslim slave or a Jew and, as they were talking about Jews, many among them who were great enemies of Israel argued that it must have been the Jews. They told the others that in many parts of Christendom, and principally in Germany, the Jews had abducted children to offer sacrifices with their blood. Because of this unfortunate and false opinion, uproar erupted and they began to tell one another and affirm that all the Jews of that place had removed the child's heart, roasted it and consumed it.[5]

In the end, only the intervention of the King saves the Jews from a massacre. Crucially, the accusation that Jews consume the hearts of children is unambiguously featured in both Espina and the Jewish sources. The reference to the Christians discussing accusations "in many parts of Christendom and principally in Germany" suggests an awareness in Castile of the wider child murder libel in Europe that indicates that it was still unusual in Spain. Based on this evidence, it appears perfectly credible that the discovery of a murdered Christian child's body in northern Castile during in the 1450s sparked anti-Jewish rumours of a ritual murder among the Christians. Unfortunately, there is no known surviving documentary evidence, or account in contemporary histories, to confirm the reality of the accusation and any subsequent investigation that are described by Espina, Usque, and Ha-Cohen.

Espina mentions two further stories of child murder allegations in the Spanish kingdom of Castile. One, supposedly

5 Samuel Usque, *Consolação às tribulações de Israel* (Ferrara: Abraham aben Usque, 1553), fols. 193r–194v.

occurring in the town of Toro in 1457 and related to Espina by the bishop of Salamanca, alleged that Jews attempted to seize two Christian children and, capturing one, rapidly sliced off pieces of his flesh and collected some of his blood before fleeing back to the nearby town of Zamora. Espina complained that no inquiries took place because of "negligence" and thus the purpose for which the Jews allegedly intended to use the Christian boy's flesh and blood remained unknown. The second, also relating to Zamora in 1457, was related to Espina by an anonymous "ordinary man" who claimed that an unnamed Jew managed to kidnap a child and take him to his house but that the screams of the boy alerted passing Christians who forced the Jew to hand over the child. The Jew, Espina asserts, claimed that he only wished to play with the boy, but the boy stated that the Jews "had seized him and wanted to kill him."[6] Given the absence of any documentary evidence about these incidents as well as the obvious antisemitic objective of his work, the stories that Espina repeated must clearly be treated with caution. Yet they offer evidence of the circulation of the child murder narrative that Jews used Christian hearts and blood for mysterious and nefarious purposes amongst both members of the church and "ordinary" people in fifteenth century Castile.

The first case of a formal trial of Jews involving the child murder libel took place in 1468 in the bishopric of Segovia in northern Spain. In this case, however, the accusation was not that Jews had murdered the child for its heart or blood. Instead, it involved the more traditional ritual crucifixion charge. The theologian Jaime Pérez of Valencia (1408–1490) is the earliest Christian source and offers a brief account of the events in Sepúlveda and Segovia:

> Likewise at that time in Sepúlveda, a Spanish town, the Jews came together on the day of Easter and killed a Christian boy with many lashes and blows with all the same reproaches [that their ancestors had] made against Christ. When news

6 For both stories see Espina, *Fortalitium fidei*, fol. 146v.

> of this crime came to the attention of Juan Arias, the bishop of Segovia, he ordered those Jews to be handed over to the secular court. Many peasants and women rose against them, hanging them and inflicting many torments against others. This was well known throughout Spain in our days.[7]

Later sixteenth- and seventeenth-century Christian sources expand slightly on the story but agree that the accusation that led to the execution of over a dozen Jews was that of a child crucifixion. A little-known fifteenth-century rabbi living in Castile, Joseph ibn Ṣaddiq de Arévalo, mentions the martyrdom of eight Jews from Sepúlveda around the same time but does not specify the nature of the accusation levelled against Jews in Sepúlveda.[8] The trials and executions in Segovia marked the first known instances in the Iberian Peninsula in which the authorities prosecuted Jews for the accusation that they had ritually crucified a Christian child. They were not the last. Over two decades after the trials and executions in Segovia, the accusation of ritual murder resurfaced in the most infamous of all Iberian ritual murder cases: that of the Holy Child of La Guardia during the reign of the "Catholic Monarchs" Isabel of Castile and her husband Fernando of Aragon.

The case of the child murder libel of La Guardia began with the arrest of a man named Benito García in the northern Castilian town of Astorga in June 1490. Benito García was a *converso*, meaning that he was the descendant of Jews who had converted to Christianity. His arrest occurred while he was returning back to his home in the village of La Guardia in central Spain from a pilgrimage to the shrine of Santiago de Compostela in northwestern Spain. The cause of the arrest was the discovery of a consecrated host in his baggage. Jews had long been accused of secretly stealing consecrated hosts

---

7 Jaime Pérez de Valencia, *Commentum in psalmos*, no foliation in the original text (fol. 190v).

8 Adolf Neubauer, *Mediaeval Jewish Chronicles and Chronological Notes* (Oxford: Clarendon, 1887), 99.

and sacrilegiously desecrating them throughout Western and Central Europe so that it is hardly surprising that a *converso* likewise came under the suspicion of harbouring the same designs. The arrest attracted the attention of the Inquisition, established by the papacy a decade earlier in the Spanish kingdom of Castile at the behest of Queen Isabel in order to hunt down all *conversos* suspected of secretly practising Judaism ("judaizing"). The prosecution of Benito fell within its jurisdiction and he was duly transferred to its jails in the town of Ávila. Fortunately for historians, many of the original trial documents have survived as well as a late sixteenth-century hagiography of Rodrigo de Yepes with the verbose title of *Historia de la muerte y glorioso martyrio del Sancto Innocente, que llaman de la Guardia, natural de la ciudad de Toledo. Con las cosas procuradas antes por ciertos Iudios, haste q[ue] al Sa[n]to Innocente crucificaro[n]: y lo sucedido después* (Madrid 1583). From these it is possible to reconstruct in considerable detail both the child murder narrative as well as the course of the investigations and trials.

The transformation of the affair from one of alleged host desecration to one of alleged host desecration *and* ritualized child murder took place during the interrogation of Benito García. Under torture, the inquisitors extracted a confession from the *converso*. This confession went much further than host desecration as Benito "revealed" the existence of a "Jewish plot" in La Guardia to kill all the Christians of Spain. The alleged conspirators, including unconverted Jews, were named, arrested and interrogated in turn, resulting in more confessions extracted under duress. These confessions led to the elaboration of a child murder narrative that has unique elements.

The narrative that emerged in what became known as the case of "the Holy Child of La Guardia" mixed elements from the crucifixion murder narrative, the host desecration accusation, and the association of Jews and black magic (see Figure 4). The Jews and *conversos* had conspired, the inquisitors alleged, to kidnap a young child in the city of Toledo in 1489 and murder it on the cross after a parody of the trial

Figure 4. The Martyrdom of the Holy Child of La Guardia. Image from Antonio de Guzmán, *Historia del inocente trinitario el Santo Niño de la Guardia* (Madrid: En la Imprenta de Diego Martinez Abad, 1720). Biblioteca Nacional de España, Madrid INVENT/30072, http://bdh-rd.bne.es/viewer.vm?id=0000184122. CC BY-SA 4.0.

and passion of Christ. After its death, the child's heart was removed so that it could be burnt. The ultimate aim of the conspirators was supposedly to mix the ashes of the heart with a consecrated host to concoct a potion that would kill all the Christians of the Iberian Peninsula.

The story of a plot to use black magic to kill all the Christians of Spain is strikingly similar to an oral legend recorded decades before by the anti-Jewish polemicist Alonso de Espina. Based on "what I have repeatedly heard, many times, from numerous people who are worthy of credit," the tale recorded by Espina involves an almost identical plot in which the Jews of France seek to kill all the Christians of that kingdom by creating a magical potion mixing a consecrated host and the heart of an innocent Christian child. In Espina's story, the Jews are fooled into accepting the heart of a pig instead of that of a Christian child and the potion causes a mass of pigs to die rather than the Christians.[9] The similarities are so striking that it is hard not to conclude that the child murder narrative of La Guardia was directly derived from this earlier anti-Jewish folktale.

Another remarkable aspect of the legal affair of the "Holy Child" of La Guardia is that it proceeded without any evidence that the murdered child actually existed. In other cases, such as those of Norwich or Trent, it was the discovery of the corpse of a child that led to the formulation of an accusation against local Jews. In the case of La Guardia, however, the inquisitors were unable to find either a body or even identify a distraught mother searching for a missing son. They brought one of the accused to the countryside outside La Guardia to identify an alleged burial place but the location indicated, a hole in the ground, contained neither body nor blood nor any other evidence such as a child's clothing. Far from being a problem for the Inquisition, the absence of a body was itself turned into "evidence." The disappearance young martyr's body was interpreted a sign

9 Espina, *Fortalitium fidei*, fol. 143v.

of God's favour to the "martyred" child and part of His mysterious plan. Remarkably, the inquisitors did not even know the alleged victim's name. In the popular cult that later emerged, the boy was variously called Juan or Cristobal (also Cristóbalito, i.e., "little Cristobal") and his mother was given the name of Mary. The names Cristobal and Mary were clearly intended to reinforce the parallels between the passions of the child and Christ, but the lack of clarity was an issue that caused embarrassment to later would-be hagiographers. Finally, the allegation that Benito García was carrying the remains of the child's heart in his luggage alongside a consecrated host was not substantiated as no physical evidence of this was discovered in the luggage.

Despite contradictions and the absence of physical evidence, the confessions effectively doomed the *conversos* and Jews arrested by the Inquisition. The Inquisitors pronounced them guilty and condemned them to be burned at the stake in November 1491 in the town of Ávila. Involving both Jews and *conversos*, the affair was a godsend to those ecclesiastics who argued that the continued toleration of Jews in Spain hindered the assimilation of *conversos*. The Inquisitor General, Tomás de Torquemada, appears to have publicized the affair widely by circulating copies of the sentence of Benito García to other churchmen, in one case even translating it into Catalan. The affair heightened anti-Jewish sentiment and the Jewish community of the town of Ávila, complained to the Crown that the Christian population was so "scandalized" by "the sentencing by the Inquisition of the town of Ávila of certain heretics and Jews residing in La Guardia" that at least one Jew was stoned by the Christian populace.[10] A century later, the Toledan inquisitor Luis de Páramo would claim that it was a major factor in moving Queen Isabel and King Fernando to order the expulsion of the Jews from their kingdoms a little

---

10 Carolyn Salomons, "A Church United in Itself: Hernando de Talavera and the Religious Culture of Fifteenth-Century Castile," *Catholic Historical Review* 104, no. 4 (2017): 654n57.

over four months later in March 1492.[11] The actual edict of expulsion does not mention the trials or the affair at La Guardia but does make it clear that the monarchs had come under intense lobbying by "the Inquisitors and many other religious persons" to expel the Jews in order to tackle the "judaizing" of the *conversos*.

Where does the child murder narrative of the "Holy Child" of La Guardia fit within the wider European context? Iberian churchmen were certainly aware of child murder accusations elsewhere in Europe. In the mid-fifteenth century, the polemicist Alonso de Espina refers to some in his work *Fortalitium fidei*. In the 1480s, the theologian Jaime Pérez de Valencia referred to the cases of Richard of Pontoise in the twelfth century and Simon of Trent in 1475 "a case famous in all of Italy, Germany and France." Whilst Jaime Pérez de Valencia notes that the boy was "crucified," he does not mention the allegation that the Jews had collected the boy's blood. The only explicit reference to a blood libel in the medieval Iberian Peninsula is to be found in a Jewish source, the *Sceptre of Judah* of Solomon Ibn Verga, who was among those expelled from Spain in 1492. Ibn Verga narrated an incident in which a wise and pious King named Alfonso (almost certainly Alfonso X) tells a Christian scholar named Thomas that the Jews are accused by some of his subjects (including a bishop) of collecting the blood of a Christian for the rituals of their Passover holiday. When a crowd of Christians enters the king's court and accuses the Jews of murdering a Christian whose body has been found in order to use his blood for ritual purposes, the scholar intervenes and exposes the blood libel allegation as a fraud motivated by anger at Jewish usury, concluding "do not follow nonsense and be infected by it." In another instance, Ibn Verga claims to have "heard that in Spain some people claimed that they had found a dead boy in the house of a Jew and that his heart had been

11 Luis de Páramo, *De origine et progressv officii Sanctae Inquisitionis, eiusque, dignitate & vtilitate* (Madrid: Ex Typographia Regia, 1598), 166.

extracted from his body to celebrate Passover." Ibn Verga was clearly repeating one or more oral stories circulating in Iberian Jewish communities and there is no documentary evidence to confirm the existence of these accusations and stories (Soyer, 323–24).

It is the notion that the Jews killed Christian children to collect and use their hearts, rather than their blood, that appears to characterize the anti-Jewish child murder narrative in Spain. This suggests an entrenched association of Jews and black magic. For the polemicist Espina, the notion that Jews could murder a Christian child to use its heart for dark rituals was commensurate with their tendency to practise black magic:

> These and many other acts of witchcraft are practised by Jews. For even though they always rebel against the idolatry of other nations, they themselves transgress God's decrees. They act as interpreters of dreams, augurers, diviners, sorcerers, magicians even though such things were prohibited in Deuteronomy 18.[12]

The human heart was believed in medieval Europe to be the location of the human soul and life force, so it is hardly surprising that the organ came to hold a special place in magical/superstitious practices and beliefs about magic. The claims made about Jews using hearts are analogous to assertions made against witches in the north of the Iberian Peninsula, more particularly the Basque country.[13]

Accusations of "ritual murder" in the Iberian Peninsula appear to have ceased after the expulsion of the Jews from Spain in 1492. If such accusations were ever made against *conversos* after 1500 then they do not appear to have been taken seriously by the lay and ecclesiastical authorities. Early Modern hagiographers nonetheless strove to perpetuate the

---

12 Espina, *Fortalitium fidei*, fol. 143v.

13 Julio Caro Baroja, *Brujería vasca* (San Sebastián: Txertoa, 1992), 33–47.

cults of Dominguito de Val and Cristobalito de La Guardia and unsuccessfully campaigned for their official canonization.[14] Their stories featured in the antisemitic polemics of the Portuguese Vicente da Costa Mattos and the Spaniard Francisco de Torrejoncillo. To this day, despite the Vatican's crackdown on the cult of Simon of Trent, these cults endure in Spain with local processions and festivals in La Guardia and Zaragoza celebrating the "child martyrs."

14 François Soyer, "Authoritative Sources: Hagiography, Local History and the Antisemitic Child Murder Libel in Early Modern Spain," *Antisemitism Studies* 9, no. 1 (2025): 71–100.

Chapter 5

Medieval Echoes in Modern Times: The Legacy of the Child Murder Libel

In *The Myth of Ritual Murder: Jews and Magic in Reformation Germany*, historian Ronnie Po-Chia Hsia has noted how child murder libels and trials flourished in the German-speaking lands of the Holy Roman Empire "in the two generations before the [Protestant] Reformation." Nevertheless, changes in elite legal and theological discourses on child murder libels during the sixteenth century resulted in the suppression of trials when accusations arose in both Catholic and Protestant parts of the Empire. He sounds a note of caution, however, that these changes in discourse "had a limited effect on the popular perception of Jews" and that the child murder and blood libels endured in the popular imagination (Po-Chia Hsia, *Myth of Ritual Murder*, 226–30). One of the major developments to occur in the early modern period was a reform of the process of beatification and canonization brought about by the 1634 decree of Pope Urban VIII *Cælestis Hierusalem cives*. Pope Urban noted that no public honour could be bestowed to any person who had not been beatified or canonized by the Apostolic See in Rome. Even though the decree made exceptions for individuals who had been venerated "from time immemorial," in practice it discouraged the emergence of new cults of children for whose deaths and "martyrdoms" the Jews could be blamed.

The medieval legend that bloodthirsty Jewish communities kidnapped and murdered Christian children to ridicule Christianity and/or consume their blood at Passover did not disappear but rather continued to feature in antisemitic propaganda such as the 1700 work *Entdecktes Judenthum* (Judaism Unmasked) of the German orientalist Johann Andreas Eisenmenger. The memory of medieval child murder "saints" and of the blood libel was perpetuated not only by antisemitic polemics. Printed works whose primary purpose was not to spread antisemitic hatred but rather to serve as a record of Church history or hagiography also played their own significant role in this process. Two of the most influential works in this category were the continuation of the Church history of Cardinal Cesare Baronio's *Annales Ecclesiastici* by the Polish Dominican Abraham Bzowski (Latin: Bzovius) (1567–1637) and the encyclopaedic multivolume compendium of hagiographies (*Acta Sanctorum*) compiled by the Bollandist society. Alongside numerous well-known saints of the Church, the latter work included entries on Simon of Trent as well as other similar medieval "child martyrs" whose deaths were ascribed to the Jews. Historian Magda Teter has noted the lasting impact of these "authoritative sources." Their authors enjoyed a prestige within the Church denied to mere antisemitic polemicists, which lent credibility to the accusations in the minds of a Christian reader because they were "difficult to dismiss." Thus, these authors effectively turned medieval lore, legends and rumours into historical fact (Teter, 10 and 162).

In western and central Europe, the child murder libel became rare. The trial and execution of Raphael Levy in the town of Metz in Lorraine in 1669–1670 was an isolated event and courts in Italy dismissed accusations of ritual cannibalism made against Jews (see Birnbaum, *A Tale of Ritual Murder*). In other cases, however, Catholic writers eager to establish saintly cults popularized medieval folk legends of child murder by Jews. In Austria, for example, the folk story of the alleged murder by Jews of a fifteenth-century boy named Andreas Oxner (also known as Anderl von Rinn), gained traction, and he became the object of local veneration in the seventeenth century.[1] The story in Eastern Europe was very

1 Judith Dengler, "Die tirolische Legende vom 'Anderl von Rinn':

different, especially in the Polish–Lithuanian Commonwealth, where blood libel accusations and even trials of Jews began at the end of sixteenth century and continued into the eighteenth century. A Polish priest who had visited Trent during a pilgrimage to Rome, for instance, played a major role in the accusation that the Jews of the town of Sandomierz had murdered a Christian child to consume its blood and the trial that followed it between 1710 and 1713. Prosecutions of Jews for alleged child murders became a recurring phenomenon, with cases occurring in Poznań (1736–1740), Zasław (1747), Markowa Wolica (1753), Jampol (1756), Wojsławice (1761), and Grabie (1774–1775). The decline of accusations in Poland during the later eighteenth century was in a large measure the result of legal and cultural transformations in the Polish government. Nevertheless, accusations continued east of Poland, in those areas of Imperial Russia known as the "Pale of Settlement," where accusations and even occasional trials took place in the early nineteenth century (see Avrutin, *The Velizh Affair*).

The attitude of the papacy towards the blood libel prior to the second half of the twentieth century was characterized by ambiguity. The leaders of the Jewish communities in Poland responded to the cases outlined above by unsuccessfully petitioning the pope in order to obtain a clear condemnation of the accusation. The attitude of the "Enlightenment Pope" Benedict XIV (1740–1758) was particularly ambivalent. Before becoming Pope Benedict XIV, Cardinal Prospero Lorenzo Lambertini authored a multi-volume book in the 1730s on the beatification of "servants of God" and the canonization of the beatified. Cardinal Lambertini opposed the canonization of young children like Simon of Trent, supposedly killed by Jews "in hatred of Lord Christ." His opposition to such canonizations hinged on the issue of whether or not small children could make the conscious choice to become

Andreaskult und Wallfahrtskirche," *historia.scribere* 10 (2018): 211–40.

martyrs but he did not question the validity of the belief that Jews murdered children in religiously motivated killings (Lambertini did not pronounce himself in this work on the alleged consumption of Christian blood). Accordingly, once Lambertini became Pope Benedict he authorized the beatification of the blood libel "victim" Anderl Oxner von Rinn in 1752 yet still refused to canonize the boy three years later. He justified his decision by arguing that while the boy could have been killed "out of hatred" of the Christian faith, (Benedict again did not refer explicitly to blood), he was nonetheless still too young to have made a conscious decision to become a martyr.

Reacting to the urgent pleas of Polish Jews, the Holy Office of the Inquisition in Rome began an investigation to determine the truth behind the blood libel, "based on the claim that their famed unleavened bread is adulterated with human blood, especially that of Christians." It commissioned Cardinal Lorenzo Ganganelli to research the claim and compile an internal report. Ganganelli examined both the past condemnations of medieval popes and theologians as well as the arguments put forward by proponents of the blood libel, attacking both the authority and credibility of the latter. Nevertheless, Ganganelli refused to question the veracity of the legends of Simon of Trent and Anderl von Rinn, which is probably not surprising given that the cults of both "boy martyrs" had been recognized by the papacy. Disingenuously, Ganganelli dismissed both cases as murders committed "in hatred of the faith" and not as the "blood accusations" that they were. His cautious conclusion was that it was impossible to use either case to argue that the blood libel "is a maxim, either theoretical or practical, of the Jewish nation; for two isolated events are not enough to establish a certain and common axiom." Ganganelli's report was completed after the death of Pope Benedict and not intended to constitute an official response to the blood libel. It was not publicized until the twentieth century (for an English translation of the report see Roth, *The Ritual Murder Libel and the Jew*).

A new wave of sensational trials involving Jews accused of kidnapping and murdering Christian children in order to harvest their blood began in the nineteenth century. The Jewish communities on the Island of Rhodes and in the Syrian city of Damascus were targeted by blood libels in 1840. Unusually, the alleged victims in the "Damascus Affair" were not children but rather a pair of missing adult males: a Franciscan friar and his Muslim servant. Extensive coverage in the press, the intervention of Jewish community leaders in Britain and France and diplomatic pressure from Britain resulted in the release of the Jewish prisoners (see Frankel, *The Damascus Affair*).

The economic, political, social, and cultural transformations in nineteenth-century Europe witnessed the emancipation of Jews in parts of the continent and the rise of an acculturated Jewish middle class. It also led to debates and questions about the place of Jews in the modern European nation state (the "Jewish Question") and the rise of a "modern" antisemitism that drew heavily upon racial science and racial theories that rejected Jews as alien and non-European. Nineteenth-century antisemites across Europe were both ethno-nationalists and Christians who demanded the abrogation of the civil rights of Jews as well as the severe limitation of their participation in politics, society, and the economy. They openly embraced conspiracy theories presenting Jews as a threat to non-Jews. Jews were portrayed as controlling capitalist economies and possessing no loyalty to the nation states in which they resided (and of which they were often citizens). Antisemites also associated Jews with the growth of organizations like Freemasonry and socialist or communist political movements seeking to subvert Christian society. Unsurprisingly, antisemites readily sought historical justifications for their position. Far from disappearing or being replaced, the blood libel found a place in this "modern" antisemitism, alongside other conspiracy theories.

A succession of high-profile trials of Jews accused of murdering children to collect their blood took place between 1882 and 1913. These were the Tiszaeszlár affair in Hungary (1882), the Xanten case in Germany (1892), the Hilsner trial in Bohemia (1899–1900), and the Mendel Beilis trial in Kiev (1911–1913), then part of the Russian Empire. These trials were not the only instances of the child murder libel accusation in modern Europe as others occurred in Eastern Europe. What makes these four trials stand out, however, is that they took place in public courts with judges and juries and attracted an enormous media interest in Europe and beyond. Journalists wrote sensationalized reports of the alleged crimes and courtroom proceedings for their readers. Editors and commentators likewise published strident editorials and opinion-pieces attacking or defending the blood libel. Sceptics of the accusation and defenders (both Jewish and non-Jewish) of Jews and Judaism reacted with dismay. The French orientalist Ernest Renan was one observer who, prompted by the Tiszaeszlár accusations, took to the press to express his views in a column published in German by the Viennese newspaper *Neue Freie Presse* on December 24, 1882, and later in French by the *Revue des études juives* the following year:

> Among all the calumnies that have served to feed hatred and fanaticism, the one that accuses Jews of murders destined to provide food for bloody feasts is assuredly the most absurd. One of the characteristic traits of the Jewish religion is the ban on the consumption of blood by men. ... And some would claim that the zealous Jew, who would die of hunger and suffer martyrdom rather than consume a piece of meat that has not been drained of blood [through kosher slaughter], consumes blood in a religious festival! This claim is monstrously inept. I am convinced that not a single account of these alleged bloody festivals is real. If such a crime were real, the culprit would be flouting all the rules of Judaism .... Human imagination is not very original when it comes to calumnies. The fable of a mysterious feast of human blood has always been the weapon used against those groups victimized by blind prejudice. Such a calumny was the cause of deplorable persecutions against [early] Christianity. Surely, Passover is innocent of such a charge just as the communal meals of early Christians were not

> tainted by such an abomination. It would be worthy of Christianity to prevent others from being accused of the same odious libel that once targeted it so unjustly.[2]

The outcomes of these trials varied. In the Tiszaeszlár and Xanten cases, the accused were eventually acquitted and released. In the Hilsner trial, on the other hand, the court found the defendant guilty and passed a death sentence (later commuted to a life sentence). The trial of Mendel Beilis ended with a mixed verdict: the acquittal of the accused but the all-Christian jury determined that the victim had indeed been the victim of a Jewish "ritual murder" (just not one personally committed by Beilis himself). One antisemitic commentator writing in reaction to the verdict reflects the way in which antisemites perceived it as a vindication of the blood libel:

> It's over. The court has acquitted Beilis. But the court has accused all kikes for using Christian blood. The kikes exult ... in the acquittal of Beilis. The kikes ignore the circumstances, you see, that the murder of [the boy] Andriusha was a ritual killing, carried out with the aim of using Christian blood. I don't know whether the kikes would have preferred the acquittal of Beilis or to have him cast under a shadow of guilt for all time. The torturers of Christian children exult, but their criminality has been proven with exhaustive clarity by the court (translated by Weinberg, 165).

Even when the defendant was acquitted, however, the result was often rioting (such as in Hungary following the Tiszaeszlár trial) and claims by antisemites that the acquittal was the result of Jewish interference and/or corruption. In central and eastern Europe, the child murder libel retained its power as an element of antisemitic discourse with the ability to mobilize Christian mobs. The disappearance of a Christian child or teenager and a mere rumour that the Jews must be

---

2 *Neue Freie Presse*, no. 6585 (December 24, 1882): 5; *Revue des études juives* 6, no. 11 (1883): 155–58.

responsible for it could unleash anti-Jewish violence. In the West Prussian town of Konitz, the Prussian government had to dispatch a regiment of soldiers to avoid an anti-Jewish riot after rumours accused a local Jewish butcher of ritually murdering a teenager whose corpse was found dismembered in 1900. Far to the south, in the Moldovan capital of Kishinev, then part of the Russian Empire, similar rumours initiated a full-scale massacre that led to the death or injury of hundreds of Jewish residents in 1903. As far away as the city Shiraz in Iran, rumours that Jews had murdered a Muslim girl "for her blood" caused an outbreak of violence in October 1910 that left a dozen Jews dead and dozens more injured.[3]

The late nineteenth and early twentieth century blood libel cases differ from those of the medieval period in the way that antisemites rationalized the blood libel through the prism of modern science. The medieval notion that Jews crucified the children and parodied the Passion of Christ disappeared to be replaced by what Hillel Kieval has described as a "disenchanted" narrative more suited to the realities of nineteenth-century European society (Kieval, *Blood Inscriptions*, 216–28). The new German term *Ritualmord* ("ritual murder") was coined in 1882 by the Hungarian parliamentarian and antisemite Géza von Ónody. It lent credibility to the blood libel by co-opting the term "ritual," a key concept in the exploration of religious or social practices in nineteenth-century academic anthropological thought. Supporters of the claim that Jews killed children to consume their blood at religious festivals presented the accusation alongside nineteenth-century academic historical and ethnographic studies of child sacrifice practised in ancient cultures, such as in the cult of the deities Moloch and Baal in the ancient Near East and North Africa. Antisemites further supported their claims by arguing that the practice of human sacrifice was not universal among Jews but rather an ancient practice still embraced by certain groups of obscurantist religious fanatics or "Talmudists." In

3 *Bulletin de l'Alliance Israélite Universelle* 35 (1910): 182–88.

typically florid language, one French antisemite cited numerous academic studies of child sacrifice and warned his readers that "what is worshipped in the ghetto is not the God of Moses but the abominable Phoenician [idol] Moloch, who requires children and virgins as human victims. ... Through some sort of phenomenon of regression, the medieval Jew degraded and returned to his primitive errors, abandoning himself to the primal impulses of that race and returning to human sacrifice."[4] The alleged victims of the Jews were still children but teenagers rather than toddlers. Another new aspect of the nineteenth-century blood libel trials was that prosecutors deployed the emerging field of forensic science in order to "prove" that the wounds on the corpses of children fitted with the notion that Jews must have deliberately harvested their blood. Autopsy reports became the subject of bitter disputes between prosecutors and defence attorneys. In some cases, the prosecution sought evidence that the victims had been killed in the same way that a Jewish slaughterer (*shochet*) killed animals to drain them of blood and render them kosher (Kieval, *Blood Inscriptions*).

Despite these nineteenth-century innovations, the discourse of modern antisemitic blood libels still owed much to its medieval past and looked to the Middle Ages to bolster its credibility. Nineteenth-century Catholic antisemitic authors, including numerous priests, took up and expounded the notion that the Talmud ordered Jews to murder Christian children in a wide variety of published works. Among the most notorious were the German August Rohling in his *Der Talmudjude* (1871) and *La France juive* (first published in 1886) by the Frenchman Édouard Drumont. Also noteworthy are *Le mystère du sang chez les juifs de tous les temps* (1889) by Drumont's compatriot Henri Desportes and Lithuanian Justinas. B. Pranaitis' 1892 tract *Christianus in Talmude Iudaeorum, sive, Rabbinicae doctrinae de Christianis secreta*

4 Édouard Drumont, *La France juive: Essai d'histoire contemporaine* (Paris: Marpon et Flammarion, 1886), 2:405 and 407–8.

(The Christian in the Jewish Talmud, or, the secrets of the rabbinical doctrine concerning the Christians). These works alleged that certain nineteenth-century Jewish communities were engaging in ritual murders, following Talmudic precepts and secretive ancient Jewish customs of human sacrifice. They enjoyed considerable commercial success. Édouard Drumont's *La France juive*, which laments a Jewish "take-over" of France, ran through no less than two hundred editions between 1886 and 1914. Similarly, Pranaitis' work was translated into Polish (1892), French (1892), German (1894), Russian (1911), Lithuanian (1912), Italian (1939), and English (1939). Rohling and Pranaitis both acted as expert witnesses for the prosecution in blood libel trials.

The trials of the nineteenth and early twentieth centuries did not result in the decisive debunking of the blood libel. On the contrary, they provided ammunition to antisemite propagandists. Polemicists and propagandists presented the long medieval history of the child murder accusations as evidence of its credibility. Antisemitic books and tracts printed long chronological lists of accusations and trials from the medieval period onwards to argue that there was "no smoke without fire." As early as 1866, the Austrian antisemitic polemicist Constantin Cholewa Von Pawlikowski offered his readers a list of seventy-three Jewish "human sacrifices" (*Menschenopfer*) in his work *Der Talmud in der Theorie und in der Praxis* (The Talmud in theory and in practice). This list, expanded and re-edited, featured in just about every subsequent polemical work discussing the child murder libel. Justinas Pranaitis, for example, put together an expanded list of blood libels in his infamous polemic. The anonymous author of an 1882 French-language tract on the "Jewish Question" included just such a list of child murders and expressed this belief in the significance of the medieval accusations:

> It seems impossible to us to deny that, in numerous countries from the era of the Crusades in Palestine to the sixteenth century, many murders of Christians [committed by Jews] have occurred, particularly of Christian children for ritual reasons. To support this claim, we have created a list,

> although indubitably an incomplete one because we have not been able to survey all the [medieval] chronicles .... This list is nevertheless sufficient to fulfil our goal. Even if one case or another might be open to doubt, it is nonetheless clear given the great number of accusations that it was the custom among Jews from the twelfth to the sixteenth centuries to seek out Christian children in order to sacrifice them and to use their blood in religious ceremonies.[5]

Reviewing the nineteenth-century accusations, the anonymous author's conclusion was that child "ritual murders" continued "among the lower classes of orthodox Jews, brought about by a doctrinal fanaticism." Late nineteenth-century antisemites seeking "evidence" of the veracity of the blood libel and claims about the Jewish use of Christian blood seized upon a work that allegedly first appeared in Moldova in 1803 and was supposedly written by a Greek monk who claimed to have been a convert to Christianity from Judaism and a rabbi prior to that. Published in different languages (in French in 1889, for example) and with various titles, it was cited in antisemitic works and newspaper articles as a trustworthy source despite its obscure and dubious origins (it may well be a forgery). The French Catholic newspaper *La Croix*, for example, referred to it in an article published in October 1913 and entitled "Le meutre rituel chez les juifs."

Catholic writers propounding the truth of the blood libel were doubtless encouraged by the official attitude of the nineteenth-century papacy, whose leadership did very little to restrain or criticize them, in a clear contrast with the clear condemnations of medieval popes. Worse still, some of the publications explicitly supporting the blood libel enjoyed the semi-official support of the Holy See. The *Osservatore Romano*, a newspaper widely seen as the Vatican's mouthpiece, argued in July 1892 that Jews murdered Christians "to use their blood in their detestable Talmudic and rabbinical

5 Anon, *La question juive: Étude historique* (Lille: de Brouwer, n.d.), 55–56 and 87.

rites" and repeated this accusation in 1899.[6] In January 1893, the Jesuit biweekly periodical *Civiltà Cattolica*, published with the support of the papacy, featured a 141-page article entitled "Jewish Morality and the Mystery of Blood" ("La morale Giudaica e Il Mistero del Sangue"), published on January 10, 1893. Its fiercely antisemitic author, the Jesuit Father Rondina, argued that Jews did not follow the Bible but rather the Talmud, which encouraged them to murder Christian children. Of course, Christian writers, whether Catholic or Protestant, were not a uniform group. There emerged trenchant Christian critics of the blood libel such as the German Protestant theologian and orientalist Hermann Strack, who published a number of works in the 1890s in direct response to the blood libel in general and the *Osservatore Romano* in particular.[7] Likewise, the French priest Abbé Elphège Vacandard published a long academic essay seeking to disprove the accusation and the veracity of the medieval and early modern accusations.[8]

Perhaps unsurprisingly, such academic voices failed to silence the antisemites as the blood libel was a conspiracy theory. Conspiracy theories, in the words of Jovan Byford, "are by their very nature irrefutable. Logical contradictions, disconfirming evidence, even the complete absence of proof have no bearing on the conspiratorial explanation because they can always be accounted for in terms of the conspiracy." Proponents of the conspiracy theory will always interpret and dismiss any counter arguments as part of an attempt to cover

6 See David Kertzer, *The Popes against the Jews: The Vatican's Role in the Rise of Modern Anti-Semitism* (New York: Knopf, 2001), 162 and 218.

7 Hermann Strack, *Der Blutaberglaube bei Christen und Juden* (Munich: Beck, 1891) and *Der Blutaberglaube in der Menschheit, Blutmorde und Blutritus zugleich eine Antwort auf die Herausforderung des "Osservatore Cattolico"* (Munich: Beck, 1892).

8 Abbé Elphège Vacandard, "La question du meurtre rituel chez les juifs," *Études de critique et d'histoire religieuse* 3rd ser., 2nd edn. (Paris: Lecoffre, 1912), 311–77.

it up and even present it as evidence of its veracity.[9] Furthermore, the ambiguous position of the papacy in relation to the blood libel trials and the "Jewish Question" more generally hindered the efforts of Catholic opponents of the blood libel. During the trial of Mendel Beilis in 1911–1913, Pope Pius X maintained a steadfast silence despite numerous appeals for an intervention and the papacy only released the report of Cardinal Ganganelli after lobbying by Lord Rothschild.[10] This lack of papal action created a vacuum in which Catholic newspaper editors in Europe and beyond felt free to publish and republish blood libel claims and attacks on Jews.

While the papacy maintained an ambiguous silence, some antisemitic propagandists of the Nazi Party in Germany eagerly embraced the blood libel. The weekly Nazi tabloid *Der Stürmer*, edited by the fanatical Jew-baiter Julius Streicher, ran a number of sensationalized stories on unsolved deaths that accused Jews of ritual murders in the 1920s and, after the Nazi rise to power in 1933, continued to refer to the libel during the 1930s and 1940s. It devoted a special edition to the topic of "the Jewish murder-plan" (*Jüdischer Mordplan*) in 1934 in which it reprinted a list of accusations and cases (expanding it to 1931). The blood libel maintained its appeal among certain elements in the Nazi party. At the height of World War II, a Nazi schoolteacher who had taken an amateur interest in the topic, Max Hellmut Schramm, published a 475-page book, an unoriginal compilation of previous accusations and antisemitic rationalizations, entitled *Der jüdische Ritualmord: Eine historische Untersuchung* (Jewish Ritual Murder: A Historical Investigation). In May 1943, the head of the SS, Heinrich Himmler, took a particular interest in the blood libel, seeing it as a means to inflame antisemitic hatred outside of Germany and facilitate the deportation of Jews to extermina-

9 Jovan Byford, *Conspiracy Theories: A Critical Introduction* (London: Palgrave, 2011), 36.

10 Giuseppe M. Croce, "L'affaire Beilis vue de Rome," *Nuova rivista storica* 86, no. 3 (2002): 561–82.

tion camps. With the support of the Nazi government, nineteen thousand copies of Schramm's work were published, although the collapse of Nazi Germany in 1945 limited its impact. Whilst the blood libel was a major element of modern antisemitism, it is important to recognize that antisemites were not a monolithic group and that it did not feature in all modern antisemitic propaganda. It does not feature, for example, in the most infamous forgery seeking to claim that there was a Jewish plot to take over the world: the Russian *Protocols of the Elders of Zion* or in many later Nazi works. In April 1943, the press chief of the Nazi regime Otto Dietrich issued a directive on the blood libel to German journalists that reveals concerns about the way that it could undermine the "seriousness" of antisemitic propaganda:

> It is necessary to make it clear to German readers that the Jewish ritual murders are not fairy tales invented by enemies of the Jews but hard, proven reality. ... The ritual murder is the continuation of human sacrifice, which was never completely given up by Jewry. We will avoid sensational make-up and unnecessary boldness, which only appeals to the readers' desire for sensation and can only damage the seriousness of this matter (O'Brien, 37–38).

The blood libel did not disappear with the death of the Nazi regime and the exposure of the horrors of the Holocaust. Rumours and accusations of child murders by Jews resurfaced rapidly in Poland in the immediate aftermath of the Second World War. The leadership of the post-war Polish Catholic Church remained hostile to Jews and refused to intervene to rein in antisemitic attacks and rumours. In July 1946, the claim that a group Jewish Holocaust survivors had detained a young boy in the basement of a building in the town Kielce sparked a full-scale riot. An enraged crowd stormed the building, which actually had no basement, and then murdered forty-two Jewish men, women and children. Investigations conducted in the aftermath of the killings recorded that members of the mob explicitly endorsed the child murder libel with cries such as "Down with the Jews, kill them, because they catch Polish children and torture them cruelly!" or "The Jews are in power and that's why they murder our children!"[11] The Papacy, for its part, took no immediate public action to condemn the blood libel after 1945 and only suppressed the cult of Simon of Trent in Italy in 1965, when the Second Vatican Council redefined relations between the Catholic Church and Jews. For its part, the cult of Anderl von Rinn in Austria was only suppressed by the local bishop in the 1980s in the face of fierce local opposition.

Despite scepticism expressed by some antisemites, the child murder libel still survives in a variety of different contexts at the start of the twenty-first century. Some conservative or ultra-traditionalist Catholics who reject the Second Vatican Council still embrace antisemitism and ignore the suppression of the cults of uncanonized children whom they continue to believe were "martyred" by Jews. Since 2007, antisemites have seized upon a book published in Italian and entitled *Pasque di sangue: Ebrei d'Europe e omicidi rituali* (Bloody Passovers: The Jews of Europe and Ritual Murders) as further "proof" of the veracity of the blood libel. Written by Israeli historian Ariel Toaff, who claimed that Ashkhenazi Jews used dried human blood for magical purposes, the work serves much the same purposes that the 1803 work allegedly written by a Jewish convert did in the nineteenth and early twentieth centuries (Johnson, *Blood Libel*, 129–64). Anonymous users of social media platforms continue to seek to promote the cult of "Saint Simon of Trent" and in Spain, the cults of Dominguito and the Holy Child of La Guardia are still tolerated by the Spanish Church (see Chapter 4). As recently as 2020, Italian Catholic artist Giovanni Gasparro caused a media furore by uploading pictures of a painting created for a private commission entitled "The Martyrdom of St. Simon of Trent for Jewish Ritual Murder" in which monstrous ste-

11 J. Tokarska-Bakir, "Cries of the Mob in the Pogroms in Rzeszów (June 1945), Cracow (August 1945), and Kielce (July 1946) as a Source for the State of Mind of the Participants," *East European Politics and Societies* 25, no. 3 (2011): 553–74.

reotyped Jews torture an infant. Bishop Ambrogio Spreafico, the president of the Bishops' Commission for Ecumenism and Dialogue of the Italian Conference of Catholic Bishops, unambiguously condemned the painting, responding that "we Catholics must comply with the Magisterium of the Church and definitively suppress such antisemitic regurgitations."[12] Finally, as a result of the Arab–Israeli conflicts, the blood libel has found a new audience in the Islamic world where the image of the vampirical Jew drinking human blood has found a place alongside other stereotypes and conspiracy theories.

12 *SIR* (information agency of the Italian Episcopal Conference), April 2, 2020. www.agensir.it/chiesa/2020/04/02/a-proposito-di-un-dipinto-su-simonino-di-trento/, accessed May 24, 2024.

Chapter 6

The Attempts of Historians and Sociologists to Explain the Phenomenon

From the twelfth to the twentieth century, Christians in very different geographical and social contexts have believed that Jews secretly conspire to kidnap Christian children in order to torture and murder them in religiously motivated ceremonies. In the twenty-first century, this belief still appears to appeal to some ultra-traditionalist Catholics as well as other kinds of extreme antisemites. Such a remarkable and disturbing persistence across centuries raises numerous questions about the nature of the libel. Why has it been so seemingly popular? What special appeal does it have that would explain why it has survived while other medieval libels such as the host desecration and well poisoning libels had largely disappeared by the 1800s? This chapter seeks to examine the various explanatory frameworks and hypotheses that scholars have proposed to rationalize the popularity and recurrence of the medieval child murder libels. Some of these theories fit specific cases and it is difficult to apply them generally to all cases. This chapter then proceeds to ask whether the child murder libel might be better understood if we study it as a folkloric belief or as a conspiracy theory.

At the heart of the child murder libel's popular resonance is undoubtedly the powerful emotions of fear, disgust, and anger. The anxiety that the abduction and murder of defenceless children provokes in societies in general and among parents in particular are evident in the huge, sensationalized attention that violent child deaths receive in the present-day media. This societal fear and the disgust caused by the violent death of a child, especially if that death is alleged to have been preceded by torture or other forms of abuse, is easily translated into anger that can be directed at a group designated as collectively responsible for the outrage in the form of rumours or more concrete accusations. Pagans in the Roman Empire, for instance, cast accusations of child sacrifice and cannibalism (alongside sexual crimes) against Christians. The child murder libel against Jews, however, has not only endured over centuries but has evolved considerably over time, developing some new characteristics and adapting to particular social and cultural environments. To understand the medieval child murder libel against the Jews, it is important to discuss the wider religious and cultural trends that might have played a role in its inception and perpetuation.

Twentieth-century historians and scholars seeking to explain the causes of the "ritual murder" and blood libels have put forward a range of different explanatory theories and frameworks. These theories have often sought to psychoanalyze the believers in order to explain the libel's appeal to individuals and communities. The Viennese Freudian psychoanalyst Theodor Reik, for example, accounted for the blood libel as the displacement of Christian guilt at having consumed Christ during the Mass and "the projection onto the Jews of the Christians' own hostile and murderous desires against the Saviour."[1] Another exponent of psychoanalytic theory, Ernst Rappaport, devoted an entire book to psychoanalyzing anti-Judaism. In a chapter devoted to the child murder libel, Rappaport argued that the blood libel constituted a case of "repetition compulsion" caused by the "persistence of doubt" among Christians about the doctrine of transubstantiation and the crucifixion of Christ. For Rappaport, this led Christians to seek substantiating evidence of these doctrines through the child murder accusations. Similarly, folklorist

1 Theodor Reik, *Der Eigene und der Fremde Gott Zur Psychoanalyse der religiösen Entwicklung* (Leipzig: Internationaler Psychoanalytischer Verlag, 1923), 129.

Alan Dundes has posited that the blood libel is a "projective inversion" in which Christians' feelings of guilt about the consumption of the consecrated host and wine caused them to project their anxieties upon Jews and to accuse them of ritualized cannibalism. Not strictly psychoanalytical in nature but still within the realm of psychohistory, Magdalene Schultz has connected the origins of the child murder libel with changing attitudes towards children in Christian Europe and Christian feelings of guilt at the abandonment and death of children. Finally, British historian Cecil Roth has explained the origins of the accusation as triggered by Christian misperceptions of the Jewish festival of Purim (Dundes, 261–360). Israeli historian Israel Yuval, for his part, has controversially sought to argue that the libels have their origin in a Christian reaction to the massacres and mass-suicides of Jews during the eleventh and twelfth-century crusades. Yuval speculates that these resulted in the Christian belief that Jews sought to commit acts of ritual vengeance on Christian children.[2] Whilst certainly thought provoking, all these claims remain largely hypothetical and too simplistic to explain the history of such a complex phenomenon as the child murder libel. Moreover, given the nature of the surviving medieval evidence, these psychoanalytical theories appear impossible to prove empirically and cannot be anything more than interesting speculations. Roth's claim about the connection between the child murder libel and Christian misperceptions of Purim might fit with a specific case such as the accusation made at Blois in 1171, but it does not help account for most of the other medieval (or even modern) accusations.

Rather than seeking to psychoanalyze the motives of individuals who lived centuries ago, many modern historians have focused instead on the wider religious, social, and cultural factors that may explain the various permutations of the child murder libel. Historians of the Church and Jew-

2 Israel Yuval, "Vengeance and Damnation, Blood and Defamation: From Jewish Martyrdom to Blood Libel Accusation" [in Hebrew], *Zion* 58 (1993): 33–96.

ish–Christian relations agree that social-religious changes in the twelfth and thirteenth centuries resulted in the growth of various anti-Jewish libels. The rise of the host desecration libel, for instance, coincided with debates among churchmen and theologians about the presence of Christ in consecrated hosts and the development of Eucharistic devotion into an important part of Christian popular piety. Similarly, the veneration of sacred, miraculous images of Christ and the Virgin Mary proliferated in Western Europe and was accompanied by the rise of accusations that Jews deliberately sought out and desecrated such images and crucifixes in a quasi-ritualistic fashion. In the context of the child murder libel, it is possible to see a particularly significant shift in the focus of popular piety from the triumphant Christ (*Christus triumphans*) to the suffering Christ (*Christus patiens*), who endured physical torment during his Passion. This was a new form of affective piety anchored in devotion to Christ in his human form, with a particular emphasis on his sufferings on the Cross. Just as the first accusations emerged and spread, Western Christian artworks depicting the Passion began to emphasize the role of Jews, with facial expressions contorted by hatred, as tormentors and "Christ-killers." The notion that Jews re-enacted the Passion of Christ on innocent children thus fitted into a wider theological context and this may help explain the relatively rapid spread of the notion of the ritual crucifixion of children by Jews from England to other parts of continental Europe. Whilst individual accusations may have had a specific context, the notion that Jews sought to crucify and murder Christian children to fulfil a secret religious ritual seems to underpin most of the early child murder libels. This is found clearly expressed in Thomas of Monmouth's hagiography of William of Norwich (see Chapter 1) as well as many other subsequent sources. In the thirteenth-century, the English chronicler Matthew Paris represented ritual crucifixion as a common Jewish practice (see Chapter 2), and the thirteenth-century Austrian poet Seifried Helbling, for example, put it succinctly in one of his works: "In every year it happens still, the Jews Christ's passion offer, when a Christian they kill" ("Ez bringent noch alliu jâr; die juden Kristes marter dar; ein kristen sie mordent").[3]

In addition to the development of affective piety focusing on Christ's Passion and Eucharistic devotion, the twelfth century also witnessed a revival in the cult of child martyrs. The story of the Holy Innocents—the male infants whom the Bible claims King Herod ordered to be murdered by his soldiers in an attempt to kill the Christ child—predated the twelfth century by many centuries but gained in popularity in the 1100s. It established a precedent for child martyrdom for those who, as the thirteenth-century compiler of saintly lives of Jacobus de Voragine claimed, had not deliberately sought to die for their faith and "confessed Christ not by speaking but by dying."[4] The Benedictine order supported and defended the cult of the Holy Innocent, as did the highly influential Cistercian Bernard of Clairvaux. The historian E. M. Rose has noted this and argued that "the accusations made against Jews in the twelfth century were closely aligned with the medieval celebration of the cult of the Holy Innocents." There is indeed clear evidence that King Philip Augustus exploited the cult of "Saint" Richard of Pontoise/Paris in the twelfth century in order to promote that of the Holy Innocents and the construction of a chapel dedicated to them in the centre of Paris. Nevertheless, it is harder to conclusively link the rising interest in the Holy Innocents with other twelfth- or thirteenth-century cults of "child-martyrs" supposedly murdered by Jews (Rose, 211–27).

The noted historian Gavin Langmuir (1924–2005) carefully considered the causes of the child murder libel in his wider work on the nature of medieval hostility to Jews, especially his two pioneering works: *History, Religion and Antisemitism*

---

3 Joseph Seemüller, *Seifried Helbring* (Halle A. S.: Buchhandlung des Waisenhauses, 1886), 101–2.

4 Robert Bartlett, *Why Can the Dead Do Such Great Things? Saints and Worshippers from the Martyrs to the Reformation* (Princeton: Princeton University Press, 2015), 176.

and *Toward a Definition of Antisemitism* (both published in 1990). Langmuir differentiated between an anti-Judaism that is a non-rational hostility to Jews or Judaism based on characteristics that Jews actually possess (which is not to say that the hostility itself is justified) and an antisemitism defined as an irrational hostility to Jews. The latter was based on characteristics that Jews do not possess and for which there is no empirical evidence. For Langmuir, tales of ritual crucifixions and cannibalism constituted important aspects of an "irrational" hostility to Jews among Christians, alongside other tales that Jews possessed horns or tails. Langmuir perceived the child murder libel as one of these irrational "chimerical fantasies" and as the result of "repressed fantasies about the crucifixion and cannibalism" among Christians. Langmuir, however, does not merely reduce the phenomenon to the fantasies of "psychologically troubled people." As Langmuir points out, the fantasy of a Jewish conspiracy to murder children might well have remained a footnote in the history of Jewish–Christian relationship. The fact that it "gradually gained acceptance" in the face of some scepticism was due not only to the wider socio-religious context of the increasingly negative way that Christians perceived Jews but also to the open or tacit support that it received from some members of the clergy, aristocracy, and even kings. Legal proceedings as well as the existence of shrines and saintly cults that seemed to enjoy the support of the local Church constituted a "social confirmation" which "then convinced many more rational people (who had already been indoctrinated in the xenophobic stereotypes) that the chimerical accusations were true." Langmuir notes that the thirteenth-century papacy rejected the blood libel but never denounced the crucifixion libels whilst in England the pious King Henry III supported the trial of the Jews of Lincoln in the 1250s (Langmuir, *Toward a Definition*, 306–9). To these examples, it is certainly possible to add the prince-bishop of Trent's notorious role in the affair of "Little Simon" in 1475 or the Catholic Monarchs Isabel and Fernando's unwillingness to impede the Inquisition's intervention in the case of the Holy Child of La Guardia. Langmuir's work offers a logical explanation, but it is not without its critics. Historian Christopher Ocker, for example, highlights emotion as a factor. Ocker posits that the child murder legends, the violence they sometimes provoked and the cults they spawned, were rooted in a popular Christianity that the papacy and many high-ranking members of the clergy often struggled to control, and which was driven by empathy with Christ, but "an empathy that did not necessarily produce the imitation of Jesus" (Ocker, 191).

The search for an explanation for the child murder libel in the evolving theology and piety of medieval Western Christendom or in theories of projection and religious doubt has thus produced a bewildering number of different explanations. These rationalizations can only go so far, however. It is important to consider the importance of folklore, that is to say the collection of traditional beliefs and myths, customs, stories, and songs passed through generations in a community by word of mouth. The blood libel in particular emerged not from a renewed focus on the crucifixion of Christ but rather from notions circulating in the Holy Roman Empire about the use of blood by Jews for medicinal or magical purposes. As such, its advent appears much more linked to popular folklore in central Europe. Inevitably, Jews featured in Christian folklore and historian Ronnie Po-chia Hsia has pointed to the significance of popular folklore and identified three "cultural themes" that underpinned the blood libel: first, Christian perceptions of Jewish magical lore; second, the belief in the potency of blood; and, third, medieval Christian "beliefs about the power of human sacrifice ... as reflected in the magical notions projected onto the sacrament of the Mass and Eucharistic sacrifice" (Po-chia Hsia, *Myth of Ritual Murder*, 6). In this respect, the blood libel appears linked to popular folklore much more than the twelfth-century child crucifixion libel. There is indeed persuasive evidence that popular folklore about Jews, blood, and the power of sacrifice lay at the root of the blood libel myth. It is noteworthy that the blood libel emerged in a specific geographical area of Europe that was culturally Germanic. Furthermore, the medieval blood libel narrative up to the end of the fifteenth century was concentrated in Germany and the Alpine areas of Europe but did not spread to culturally different spaces such as England, France and the Iberian Peninsula, where Christians accused Jews of crucifying children or of using their hearts for magical purposes but not of consuming their blood. The first blood libel case at Fulda in 1235, and the lethal violence it unleashed, seems to have been an entirely popular outburst originating in Christian fears about the Jewish use of blood for medicinal purposes. Crucially, the Fulda blood libel did not feature cannibalism during Passover. This aspect only appeared later in the Alpine regions when the libel incorporated different folkloric notions about Jewish cannibalism during Passover.

The celebrity of the cult of Simon of Trent—combining both the crucifixion and blood libels in its narrative—has probably played a role in obscuring the role that popular folkloric beliefs about alleged Jewish cannibalism played in the gradual development of the blood libel as distinct from the crucifixion libel. While comparisons between the persecution of Jews and alleged witches are contentious among historians, there are salient parallels in a range of folkloric beliefs about both groups, including the kidnapping and murder of children as well as cannibalism. The association of Jews and black magic in medieval Christian folklore doubtless assisted the spread of the blood libel in central Europe. In the twentieth century, Joshua Trachtenberg argued that the blood libel was the result of "superstition"—a term he appears to use as a synonym for folklore—and the conflation in the Christian mind "between two mythical Jews—the sorcerer and the child murderer." Trachtenberg argues that one cannot properly understand the appeal and endurance of the blood libel "unless viewed against the background of medieval superstition and seen as another expression of the Christian conviction that the Jews are the spawn of the devil, committed to destroy Christendom, both by direct murder and by indirect magical means" (Trachtenberg, 155). It is not possible to draw a direct link between accusations of child cannibalism against witches and those against Jews but it is certainly striking that the earliest accusations of Jews consuming the blood of Christian children at Passover emerged in roughly the same geographical areas where witches were accused of consuming children. It is intriguing that the accusation of cannibalism against Jews recorded by judges in Savoy in the early fourteenth century (see Chapter 2) are not dissimilar to accusations of cannibalism during Sabbaths also made against alleged witches in the Alpine region of the Valais (southwestern Switzerland) in the early fifteenth century. The recognized role played by folklore about magic and witchcraft in the rise of late medieval and early modern witch crazes and witch-hunts, underscores the significance of not ignoring folklore as a major factor in shaping the blood libel against Jews.

Looking beyond psychology and folklore, one of the ways to understand the longevity of the child murder libel and its enduring appeal is probably to examine it both as an element within a broader anti-Jewish conspiracy theory as well as a conspiracy theory itself. The philosopher Karl Popper claimed in his 1945 work *The Open Society and its Enemies* that the "conspiracy theory of society"—in essence the belief that the development of events and society is determined by secret human plots—was the result of the social and intellectual transformations that took place in Europe in the eighteenth century. Nonetheless, conspiracy theories have long been powerful social forces in the Western world as well as instruments of social control and propaganda. Social psychologist Jovan Byford has noted that conspiracy theories are characterized by a distinctive "thematic configuration, narrative structure and explanatory logic as well as by the stubborn presence of a number of common motifs and tropes."[5] Conspiracy theories are indeed narratives that share three central elements. The first is that conspiracy theories consistently accuse a group of individuals who, paradoxically, are both plotting secretly and well identified (in this case the Jews). Secondly, conspiracy theories always ascribe a malevo-

5 Byford, *Conspiracy Theories*, 4.

lent objective to the designated group, which is also allegedly secret yet clearly identified (here the abduction, torment, and murder of children). Thirdly, and finally, the narrative of conspiracy theories will detail a secret plan that the conspirators have elaborated to achieve their malevolent objective (the carefully planned abduction and then the attempt to fulfil a religious obligation and to conceal the crime afterwards).

In every one of its different forms, the anti-Jewish child murder libel follows this conspiracist framework. Conspiracy theories exercise a seductive power on their believers through the creation of an explanatory framework that revolves around simplicity and a Manichean dualism. A confusing and frightening world is rationalized by its division between the forces of good (God, the Church, and Christian society) and evil (the Devil and his human agents, including the Jews). The emotional investment of the believer in the conspiracy theory is frequently absolute as it rationalizes their entire worldview: one in which Jews, inspired by the Devil and the Talmud, conspire to murder Christian children just as they also plot to poison wells and desecrate consecrated hosts. As the previous chapters have demonstrated, this conspiracist narrative was present from the very start in the twelfth century and it is present across all the different variations of the child murder libel narrative. The hagiography of William of Norwich cast the murder as part of a much wider Jewish conspiracy secretly organized by a Jewish elite in southern France. Jews arrested and questioned under torture at Valréas in the 1240s were apparently asked to confirm that all Jewish communities in Christendom, and those in Spain in particular, murdered Christian children. Likewise, in his discussion of the child murder accusation at Pforzheim in the 1260s, the fifteenth-century Franciscan polemicist Alonso de Espina thought it necessary to inform his readers that "wherever they reside, the Jews shed Christian blood, which is now their custom."[6] In the late fifteenth century, the

6 Espina, *Fortalitium fidei*, fols. 143r–145v.

Humanist scholar Ubertino Pusculo wrote a poem dedicated to "Simon [of Trent] the Martyr" in which he traced the origins of the blood libel to a fanciful Jewish "council" held in Mesopotamia eight centuries before in which Jews, resentful of Christianity's success, "decided every year in perpetuity to seek a boy from a faithful Christ-worshipping family who was not yet seven years old and secretly destroy him by a new mode of death, so that he gave up his tender life as well as his drained-out blood" (Bowd and Cullington, 143–45). Even when there is no explicit reference to a wider conspiracy, the narrative is clear that the murder is a Jewish ritual that implicates the guilt of *all* Jews. Medieval polemicists and hagiographers did not seek to argue, as some nineteenth century antisemites did, that only a small number of Jewish religious fanatics were responsible.

The child murder libel fits within the wider medieval conspiracy theory that Jews were conspiring to undermine and destroy the Church and Christian society through acts of treason, alliances with Muslims, and the desecration of sacred images and objects. It is hardly surprising that late medieval or early modern anti-Jewish polemicists rarely discuss it in isolation but rather alongside other examples of "Jewish perfidy." The polemicist Alonso de Espina, for example, discussed cases of child murder by Jews as part of what he perceived to be a wider conspiracy against Christendom in general, and "wretched Spain" (*misera Hispania*) in particular. For Espina, these child murders are part of the "Jewish cruelties" inflicted upon Christians and he rages in his work that "the enemy is the heretic; the enemy is the Jew, the enemy is the Muslim; the enemy is the Devil."[7] A modern fascination with the occult, secret societies and alleged secret conspiracies bolstered the appeal of the child murder libel in the nineteenth century and this seems to highlight its intrinsic conspiracist nature. Modern antisemitic authors such as the Frenchman Édouard Drumont (see Chapter 5) who wrote

7 Espina, *Fortalitium fidei*, fol. 2r.

about "ritual crimes" secretly committed by Jews often also spread Judeo-Masonic conspiracy theories. Similarly, the reactionary French writer Albert Monniot is another perfect example of this trend. A close associate of Drumont and the author of a work promoting the blood libel entitled *Le crime rituel chez les juifs* in 1914, Monniot also wrote a range of sensationalist works railing against secret conspiracies and murders by Jews or Freemasons seeking to destabilize France.

Whilst it is empirically difficult to look into the minds of medieval people in order to establish precisely what they believed about the child murder libel, there can be no denying that the ecclesiastical and secular elites who supported accusations exploited it to serve their own purposes. In a number of cases—most notably Norwich in the twelfth century and Trent in the fifteenth century—it is clear that the local bishops sought to exploit the libel to create a centre of pilgrimage that would increase their prestige and help fill their coffers. It will never be known whether these bishops actually believed the accusation or were cynical opportunists. It is perfectly possible that such Christian leaders both believed the libels and were at the same time opportunists on the lookout for material gain. Like all conspiracy theories, the child murder libel could be exploited as an instrument of political propaganda and of social control because of its ability to foment "moral panics": situations in which groups of individuals—in this case Jews—are defined as threats not just to individuals but also to wider "societal values and interests."[8] The case of the Holy Child of La Guardia in the Iberian Peninsula is a case in point. As Chapter 4 has indicated, the Inquisition in the Spanish kingdom of Castile did not fabricate the accusation but took charge of the investigations and trials, helping to direct and formulate its narrative. Its intervention served to buttress its position in that kingdom in the final decade of the fifteenth century.

---

8 Stanley Cohen, *Folk Devils and Moral Panics* (St. Albans: Paladin, 1973), 9.

Finally, another key aspect of any conspiracy theory is that it is impossible to disprove it through rational reasoning. Medieval hagiographers and polemicists were well aware that child murder accusations faced scepticism or even outright disbelief. Like modern antisemitic polemicists, these medieval authors pointed to previous accusations as an argument in and of itself in the struggle to convince these sceptics. References to other, preceding accusations and cults are common in such work. In the twelfth century, Abbot Robert Torigni referred to previous English cases when discussing the events at Blois in 1171, while the fifteenth-century polemicist Alonso de Espina featured numerous examples selected from across Europe to bolster the credibility of the tales presented in his polemic. Condemnations of the blood libel by popes or emperors and the intervention of royal officials to prevent violence against Jews after the discovery of a dead child did not stop the recurrence of child murder libels in the medieval period any more than they have in the modern era. Many Christian secular rulers and the church hierarchy usually had their own reasons to intervene to stop child murder accusations. Jewish communities paid extra taxes to the royal treasury and were under the direct authority of secular rulers so that an attack on them was also an attack on that authority. Nevertheless, believers were all-too-ready to claim that the Jews, the conspirators, sought to keep their alleged crimes secret by bribing ecclesiastical and secular authorities. This is evident in the very first case, when the hagiographer Thomas of Monmouth asserted that the Jews of Norwich bribed the local sheriff to protect them and hush up the affair. The same claim of bribery appears in Richard of Devizes' account of the accusation at Winchester in 1192. In the thirteenth-century, the monk and chronicler Richer of Senones was similarly convinced that the Jews had bribed Emperor Frederick II to intervene on their behalf after the first blood libel:

> When they saw the danger coming to them, the Jews took counsel and determined to placate the Emperor with money.

> Presenting themselves to the Emperor, they blinded him with a huge sum of money so that having obtained his favour, they returned cheerfully to their dwellings. When the emperor returned to Hagenau, the Christians presented the [bodies of the] three boys to him and explained to him in detail that the Jews had killed them in such a way. To this, the emperor answered, "if they are dead, go, bury them, for they have no further use." Upon hearing this, the Christians were confused and departed from him. Thus, that hapless emperor made his lack of faith clear to all because the Jews were dismissed in peace and no justice was rendered to the Christians in such a sinister deed.[9]

Reading between the lines, Richer of Senones's account seems to be a denunciation of Frederick's 1236 edict condemning the blood libel. In the Iberian Peninsula, Alonso de Espina's account of child murders in Spain and Europe follows a similar line. When Jews are not prosecuted and punished by the Crown's officials, it is only because they have bribed and influenced judges to protect them or benefitted from the assistance of insincere Jewish converts to Christianity.

---

9 *Gesta episcoporum abbatum ducum aliorumque principum saec. XIII*, edited by Pertz, 324.

Conclusion

The history of the medieval child murder libel is the history of an idea. At its most basic, that idea is that Jews secretly kidnap Christian children in order to torture and murder them for religious reasons. Ideas, however, are not static. Different local cultural norms and religious contexts influenced and moulded the idea as it spread to new geographical areas. The result is that the idea evolved different versions over time: at first Jews were accused of abusing and crucifying children in a parody of the Passion of Christ, then this accusation was joined by the claim that Jews drained the blood of Christian children to use it for either medicinal or magical reasons. The idea that Jews consumed the blood of Christian children as part of their Passover celebrations also emerged. In Spain, one famous case saw Jews accused of killing a child not to eat its blood but to collect its heart in a demonic scheme to concoct a potion that would kill all the Christians of the Iberian Peninsula.

Tracing the history of this idea and its evolution is a challenging task for a historian. We can confidently point to its origin in twelfth-century England and follow its development but the nature of its transmission across Europe is far less straightforward. Historians have access to chronicles and hagiographies but there is little doubt that the transmission of tales of child murder by Jews often occurred via casual conversations or as stories told and retold in inns, households, churches, and monasteries across many parts of Europe. Most of the written accounts explicitly refer to the oral transmission of the child murder libel. In the twelfth century, Thomas of Monmouth claims to have heard of the conspiracy to murder Christian children from a converted Jew and, in the thirteenth century, the Dominican Thomas of Cantimpré did not hide the fact that his account of the accusation of Pforzheim was based on his conversation with two fellow Dominicans. Similarly, the polemicist Alonso de Espina credited his account of a child murder libel to "what I have repeatedly heard, many times, from numerous people who are worthy of credit" and claimed that another story he recorded had been told to him by a Jewish convert to Christianity named Emmanuel in a private conversation. Songs were also an effective way to communicate news and stories and the child murder libel was doubtless also disseminated in sung verse. Chaucer's reference to the story of Saint Hugh [of Lincoln] "slayn also / With cursed Jewes, as it is notable / For it is but a litel while ago" in *The Prioress's Tale* is probably the most famous example but there were doubtless many others. A decree seeking to stop anti-Jewish violence in Brescia in 1475 forbade peddlers who recited or sang vernacular ballads to crowds from referring to Simon of Trent (Bowd and Cullington, 14n53). We must not overlook the importance of this oral transmission. Oral transmission allows ideas to be easily adapted and modified to suit very different contexts and audiences, thus leading to their interpretation and re-interpretation over time. Furthermore, the oral transmission of stories of child murder by Jews relied on human memory and personal interpretations and this can only have assisted in the emergence of a diversity of versions of the libel. Interestingly, Jewish sources also evoke this oral transmission within Christian and Jewish communities. Samuel Usque, a descendant of Portuguese Jews forced to convert to Christianity, features a vivid account of an accusation that conveys the power of such stories to influence listeners (see Chapter 4). Writing in the sixteenth century, after fleeing the Iberian Peninsula, Solomon ibn Verga recalled a particular child murder libel story, specifying that "I did not read this but heard it said [in Spain before 1492]."[1]

The fact that belief in the medieval child murder libel still exists today offers striking evidence of its adaptability and enduring appeal among some ultra-traditionalist Catholics, who reject Vatican II and refuse to question the validity of medieval cults, or among more secular antisemites who believe that Jews consume the blood of non-Jews as part of an alleged "Talmudic" religious ritual. The libel might well meet with scepticism today just as it did in the medieval period, but the fear of child abduction and murder constitutes a powerful emotional trigger, and the nature of the narrative will always appeal to conspiracy theorists and occultists. The child murder narrative will probably continue to be adapted and repurposed to suit different contexts and audiences. Reference to it may be explicit or made through coded and suggestive language that acts as an antisemitic dog whistle, such as claims that Jews/Israelis/Zionists have a unique predilection for the killing of non-Jewish children. While antisemitism still exists, it is unlikely that the child murder libel will disappear in the age of the Internet and unmediated social media offering its users anonymity and a forum to express their hatreds freely through words or images. By presenting Jews as an existential threat, antisemites will continue to deploy the child murder libel alongside other antisemitic libels as a warrant for persecution, exclusion and even murder.

1 Solomon ibn Verga, *Shevet Yehudah*, edited by Azriel Shochat and Yitzhak Baer (Jerusalem: Bialik Institute, 1947), 126.

Further Reading

The following moderately annotated list contains various titles that are particularly relevant to anyone interested in the subject of this book and that are generally available. Given the fact that this book is aimed at an Anglophone readership, the works listed are all in English although a number of significant works also exist in Hebrew, French, German, Italian, Russian, and Spanish. Many of the original and crucial primary sources are not available in translation and have not been included here.

Avrutin, Eugene M. *The Velizh Affair: Blood Libel in a Russian Town*. Oxford: Oxford University Press, 2018.

A study of the spread and establishment of the medieval blood libel in Russia during the early nineteenth century. The book focuses on the case study of an accusation and the legal proceeding that followed in a small regional town.

Bale, Anthony. *The Jew in the Medieval Book: English Antisemitisms 1350–1500*. Cambridge: Cambridge University Press, 2006.

This interdisciplinary study explores images of Jews and Judaism in late medieval English literature and culture. It includes an interesting study of the accusation that Jews martyred a boy named Robert in the English town of Bury St. Edmunds.

Birnbaum, Pierre. *A Tale of Ritual Murder in the Age of Louis XIV: The Trial of Raphaël Lévy, 1669*. Stanford: Stanford University Press, 2012.

An analysis of a blood libel trial and subsequent execution in eastern France during the seventeenth century. Birnbaum explores the cultural, political, and personal elements that led to the medieval accusation reappearing centuries later.

Bowd, Stephen and Cullington, J. Donald *"On Everyone's Lips": Humanists, Jews, and the Tale of Simon of Trent*. Tempe: Arizona Center for Medieval and Renaissance Studies, 2012.

A study of how printed verse and prose accounts written by Renaissance humanists helped spread the cult of Simon of Trent and the blood libel against Jews. This scholarly works offers a selection of vernacular and Latin texts edited with facing translations into English as well as notes.

Chazan, Robert. "The Bray Incident of 1192: Realpolitik and Folk Slander." *Proceedings of the American Academy for Jewish Research* 37 (1969): 6–18.

A detailed study of the sources for a murder accusation brought against Jews in twelfth-century France and the context in which it occurred.

Chazan, Robert. *Medieval Stereotypes and Modern Anti-Semitism*. Berkeley: University of California Press, 1997.

A comprehensive analysis of the numerous anti-Jewish stereotypes and libels that circulated in medieval Christendom and their modern echoes.

Dundes, Alan, ed. *The Blood Libel Legend: A Casebook in Anti-Semitic Folklore*. Madison: The University of Wisconsin Press, 1991.

A useful collection of edited chapters by various authors on the child murder libels. A significant number of these feature attempts to rationalize the libel according to different theories.

Frankel, Jonathan. *The Damascus Affair: "Ritual Murder," Politics, and the Jews in 1840*. Cambridge: Cambridge University Press, 1997.

A detailed study of the blood libel accusation that targeted the Jewish community in Damascus in 1840 after the disappearance of a Franciscan friar and his servant as well as the international response that it provoked.

Hillaby, J. "The Ritual-Child-Murder Accusation: Its Dissemination and Harold of Gloucester." *Jewish Historical Studies* 34 (1994): 69–109.

An impressively detailed study of the child murder libel that emerged in the English town of Gloucester in the 1160s and what it reveals to us about the manner in which the libel spread in twelfth-century Europe.

Israeli, Raphael. *Blood Libel and its Derivatives: The Scourge of Anti-Semitism*. London: Routledge, 2012.

Examining various antisemitic libels, this volume seeks to explain the origins of the blood libel and aims to define the different ways in which its derivatives have continued to achieve acceptance in certain parts of the world today.

Johnson, Hannah R. *Blood Libel: The Ritual Murder Accusation at the Limit of Jewish History*. Ann Arbor: The University of Michigan Press, 2012.

The first book to study the modern historiography of the child murder libel and to analyze the historical debates, especially about its origins, that have emerged from the works of scholars like Gavin Langmuir, Israel Yuval, and (much more controversially) Ariel Toaff.

Kieval, Hillel J. *Blood Inscriptions: Science, Modernity, and Ritual Murder at Europe's Fin de Siècle*. Philadelphia: University of Pennsylvania Press, 2022.

This book focuses on four modern cases: the prosecutions that took place at Tiszaeszlár in Hungary (1882–1883), Xanten in Germany (1891–1892), Polná in Austrian Bohemia (1899–1900), and Konitz (1900–1902). It considers how discredited medieval beliefs came to seem once again as plausible. Kieval argues that these ritual murder trials were products of post-Enlightenment politics and culture that reframed the medieval blood libel using scientific discourse.

Langmuir, Gavin I. *Towards a Definition of Antisemitism*. Berkeley: University of California Press, 1990.

Langmuir's now classic work on the history of antisemitism, focusing on the questions: What is antisemitism? Where and when did it emerge, and why? Includes a detailed analysis of child murder libels in the twelfth and thirteenth centuries.

O'Brien, Darren. *The Pinnacle of Hatred: The Blood Libel and the Jews*. Jerusalem: Hebrew University Magnes Press, 2011.

This book provides a comprehensive history of the child murder libels against the Jews from the medieval period to today. Drawing on primary sources and documents not previously available in English, O'Brien argues for a nuanced analysis, distinguishing between crucifixion murder, plain murder, mutilation murder, blood libel, and "ritual murder."

Ocker, Christopher. "Ritual Murder and the Subjectivity of Christ: A Choice in Medieval Christianity." *The Harvard Theological Review* 91, no. 2 (1998): 153–92.

A thoughtful study of the emotional context of certain medieval anti-Jewish legends. This article examines how the stories redefined the composition of society, the link between this and popular devotion, and the paradox between religious intentions and their effects.

Po-chia Hsia, R. *The Myth of Ritual Murder: Jews and Magic in Reformation Germany*. New Haven: Yale University Press, 1988.

In this work Ronnie Po-Chia Hsia traces the rise and decline of ritual murder trials in the German-speaking lands of the Holy Roman Empire. Using a wide range of Christian and Jewish sources, Hsia examines the religious origins of the idea of child sacrifice and blood symbolism. He also reconstructs the political context of child murder trials against the Jews in fifteenth and sixteenth-century Germany.

Po-chia Hsia, R. *Trent 1475: Stories of a Ritual Murder Trial*. New Haven: Yale University Press, 1992.

A brief and accessible reconstruction of the events surrounding the discovery of the body of a young Christian child in a Jewish family's house in the town of Trent in 1475. Based on trial records, this work examines the blood libel accusation, subsequent trials and executions.

Resnick, Irven M. "Medieval Roots of the Myth of Jewish Male Menses." *The Harvard Theological Review* 93, no. 3 (2000): 241–63.

A scholarly analysis of the medieval Christian myth that Jewish males menstruated as a punishment for the role of their forefathers in the death of Christ. The myth occasionally features in accusations that Jews used the blood of Christian children as a medical remedy to cure these monthly menses.

Rose, E. M. *The Murder of William of Norwich*. Oxford: Oxford University Press, 2015.

Rose's book explores the story of William's murder and the origins of the child murder libel in Western Europe during the central Middle Ages. Rose focuses on the specific historical context and examines four "copycat" cases in England and France.

Roth, Cecil, ed. *The Ritual Murder Libel and the Jew: The Report by Cardinal Ganganelli (Pope Clement XIV).* London: Woburn, 1935.

An edition and translation of the famous eighteenth-century report into the blood libel by Cardinal Ganganelli (later Pope Clement XIV).

Soyer, François. "Jews and the Child Murder Libel in the Medieval Iberian Peninsula: European Trends and Iberian Peculiarities." *Journal of Medieval Iberian Studies* 13, no. 3 (2021): 309–30.

An article that examines the rise of the child murder libel in the medieval Iberian Peninsula and seeks to examine both the similarities with other accusations but also the ways in which it differed from the rest of Europe.

Teter, Magda. *Blood Libel: On the Trail of an Antisemitic Myth*. Cambridge, MA: Harvard University Press, 2020.

A magisterial study of the cult of Simon of Trent and the spread of the blood libel from 1475 to the present. Teter follows the surviving evidence to chart how the blood libel was internalized in Christian society and how Jews and Christians responded to accusations.

Thomas of Monmouth. *The Life and Passion of William of Norwich*. Translated and edited by Miri Rubin. London: Penguin, 2014.

An authoritative translation, edition, and analysis of the Latin hagiography *The Life and Passion of William of Norwich*, our principal source for the first child murder libel to appear in the twelfth century.

Trachtenberg, Joshua. *The Devil and the Jews: The Medieval Conception of the Jew and its Relation to Modern Anti-Semitism*. Philadelphia: The Jewish Publication Society, 1993.

A classic, if somewhat dated, work on medieval Christian antisemitism. Trachtenberg examines various libels and devotes a chapter to the child murder libel and another one to the blood libel.

Weinberg, Robert. *Blood Libel in Late Imperial Russia: The Ritual Murder Trial of Mendel Beilis*. Bloomington: Indiana University Press, 2014.

This book examines the trial of Mendel Beilis, a Jewish manager of a brick factory in Kiev who was targeted by a blood libel accusation. Accused of murdering a Christian teenage boy for his blood, Beilis was jailed and put on trial between 1911 and 1913. Weinberg analyzes the trial transcript as well as government reports and contemporary newspapers that covered the case.

Printed in the United States
by Baker & Taylor Publisher Services